MW01039832

WRITING
EFFECTIVE
ESSAYS

~

A GUIDE TO COLLEGE-LEVEL WRITING

Wesley Kisting

7290 Investment Drive Suite B
North Charleston, SC 29418

Copyright © Wesley Kisting, 2011

All rights reserved.
No part of this publication may be reproduced or transmitted
in any form or by any means without prior permission
in writing from the author.

An earlier digital edition of this guide appeared under the title
Writing Effective Essays: A Nuts and Bolts Guide.
Copyright © Wesley Kisting, 2007. All rights reserved.

Manufactured in the United States of America

ISBN-13: 978-1-461-17130-0 (paperback)

ISBN-10: 1-461-17130-X (paperback)

Table of Contents

Find Your Voice

Ideally, all students learn formal academic writing in high school. Realistically, most enter college ill-prepared for college-level writing. If you're among the latter, the formal essay probably seems like a mystifying genre. You may even believe that you're a bad writer and dread the task of writing. Perhaps you do whatever you can to avoid it, reassuring yourself that, some day—after you graduate—you will never again be forced to write.

What you may not realize is that by avoiding writing you are creating considerable grief for yourself, now and in the future. Formal writing doesn't have to be mystifying. It follows an intelligible *structure* with specific *guidelines* for presenting information in a *clear*, *concise*, and *compelling* manner. It isn't easy to learn, but it gets easier. As you learn to break the writing process down to its essential elements—the "nuts and bolts" of writing—it becomes more manageable and more rewarding. You learn to make words say exactly what you want them to say. You find your "voice".

When that happens, writing ceases to be a chore. It becomes a pleasure, a formidable tool, a liberating experience—perhaps even a necessity, like breathing. You discover that words can shout, whisper, tease, provoke, or sing. You start to understand that language is power, and begin to make its power work for you. Developing this ability is vital. No other skill set will empower or disable you more in life than your facility with language.

From High School to College

Students enter college laden with misconceptions about writing—often because high school trained them to think and write in ways that are severely inadequate by college standards. Consequently, college writing instructors expend a lot of effort trying to "deprogram" bad habits that high school writing instruction instilled.

Have students been betrayed by their high school teachers? Not exactly. High school teachers establish artificial "rules" to help students learn basic structural and stylistic features of formal writing. But later, as students develop in skill and confront more challenging writing tasks, these "rules" become more cumbersome than helpful. They may even reinforce certain deficiencies.

For example, high school teachers often forbid the "I" voice in formal writing. Yet sometimes the "I" voice is needed to qualify or contextualize your ideas—especially when describing a personal experience. The reason many high school teachers forbid references to "me," "myself," and "I" is because *most* of the time these references are unnecessary and novices tend to overuse them.

Another "rule" is to start an introduction with a broad generalization, followed by statements that become increasingly specific as they lead to the thesis. This makes the paper more accessible by gradually leading readers from the general topic to the specific argument. However, most students begin *too* broadly, with absurdly cosmic statements, such as: "Since the dawn of time, love has affected mankind," or "There are many ways to interpret a story, but only some interpretations can be supported by evidence." These claims are so generic that they convey nothing meaningful. Instead, they frustrate the reader. A good introduction should move from the general to the specific, but even the first sentence should begin to *specify* the paper's topic and scope.

Some rules learned in high school may even jeopardize your college career. An alarming number of students claim they were taught that "if you read an article, then set it aside and rephrase the ideas in your own words, they 'become' your ideas and don't need to be cited." This advice is wrong. If you follow this rule in college, you will be failed for plagiarism—possibly even expelled.

A broader problem—though not a "rule" of high school—is that too many students expect college to be similar to high school in terms of rigor. But you must work *much* harder (and be more proactive about your studies) to succeed in college. Completing the assigned work is not enough. You need to make a concerted effort to identify deficiencies in your skills and knowledge, then work to remedy those deficiencies. If you lack such initiative, or fail to devote ample time to your studies, you will falter in college or in your future career. *Now* is the time to avoid those problems by embracing college studies with the right attitude.

Your early encounters with college-level writing will likely feel exasperating, but there is purpose behind the apparent madness. Although it may seem like you are receiving mixed messages, you are actually developing a more sophisticated understanding of concepts that were previously ignored or taught to you as fixed "rules." If you keep an open mind and apply yourself diligently, college-level writing eventually rewards you with the ability to express yourself in ways that the "rules" of high school did not allow.

The College Attitude

Every semester, students ask why I am so tough on their writing. Often, they complain that they earned A's or B's in other English classes, but only receive C's or D's from me. I understand their concern, but my answer is always the same: The problem is not that I am too strict, but that others have been too lenient, resulting in severely counter-productive attitudes about learning.

Regrettably, most students believe it is more important to receive high grades than to confront challenges that demand personal growth. Yet the latter idea—a challenge that requires personal growth—is the fundamental principle of education. In the same way that physical exercise increases stamina, the mental exercise of education enhances your intellect, but only if you exercise *at the upper limits of your abilities*, outside of your normal "comfort zone." If earning an A feels easy or comfortable, or can be achieved by pulling an "all-nighter," something is very wrong. Earning an A should feel intensely challenging, sometimes even vexing; otherwise, you're not cultivating your writing skills to any significant degree. You may even be losing ground.

Other instructors may have given you high grades for a number of reasons: your effort level, your desire to learn, your improvement in a specific skill, your creativity, or your unusually good grasp of a topic. Some may have deliberately inflated your grade to "motivate" or "reward" you despite notable deficiencies in your writing. Others may have inflated grades for compassionate reasons, believing that some of your deficiencies were not entirely your fault because other factors—personal, social, economic, or educational—may have made the learning process more difficult for you than for others. These may be intelligible reasons to inflate a grade, but when they become the prevailing rationales—replacing the primary concern for *the quality of what you actually produce*—they result in a truly insidious effect: They build false confidence in your abilities, blinding you to the fact that you still have *much* to learn and that the writing for which you have been receiving A's may be judged incompetent in the professional world.

A larger problem with grade inflation is its negative effect on learning attitudes. When students describe themselves as an "A student" based on their previous education, they think they're stating a well-documented fact. Consequently, when they receive C's or D's from a college professor, it appears unfair or unkind. In actuality, the reverse is more often true: Low grades in college are usually very fair by national standards—perhaps *more* than fair, since grade inflation is rampant in college, too. Often, low grades feel jarring and unpleasant in college only because they are the first honest revelation that high school did not prepare you adequately.

Worse, the combination of grade-inflation, low standards in schools, and poor preparedness for college reinforces students' already-misguided obsession with high grades, often to the complete exclusion of rigor. But ask yourself this: Is it better to slide easily through college to discover that the professional world considers you unemployable; *or* is it better to be challenged—to struggle for awhile—and to finally emerge with well-earned skills that make you genuinely outstanding among other qualified individuals competing for the same job? The answer to this question should be obvious. If you really want to improve yourself and your value to others, you need to focus less on grades and more on embracing the challenges that education entails.

Educational Maturity

The most significant factor affecting the quality of your education is your own maturity level. Though difficult to describe, your maturity level dictates whether you thrive or fail in *any* course—especially in courses that demand rigorous practice and careful self-assessment, such as writing-intensive English courses. Unfortunately, few instructors explicitly address the subject of "college-level maturity" or how to acquire it. Instead, students struggle to develop it on their own—an experience that often breeds confusion, frustration, and resentment.

It is impossible to define educational maturity in concise terms, but I can give you an example: Sometime after my first year in college, I stopped enrolling in courses with reputations for *ease* (those I considered "safe" enough not to "endanger" my GPA) and began enrolling in courses that intimidated me because of their reputation for *rigor*. My thought process went something like this: "If I'm afraid to take this course, I must not be confident about my abilities in this subject, or maybe I'm just too lazy to see if I can meet the instructor's standards. But if I truly want to be ready for the professional world with a formidable set of skills, I need to get past these fears and face the challenge now—while someone is willing and available to teach me."

Thereafter, I deliberately enrolled in courses taught by professors with reputations for rigor. I still don't know what caused my attitude to shift in this way, but I am profoundly grateful that it did because it made a remarkable difference in my education. Yes, I did struggle more at first because the courses definitely became harder, but to my surprise and delight, their rigor also made learning far more stimulating and rewarding. I could *feel* my mind and skills expanding, yielding a deeper sense of confidence and satisfaction unlike anything I had experienced before. These rewards did not come overnight, but they did come. Then I finally understood that to "enjoy" education means something far richer and deeper than merely having "fun" playing games in class. To truly "enjoy" education is to experience that kind of satisfaction from ethical and intellectual growth that can only be felt after a tremendous personal investment of hard work, in service to high standards. *That* is educational maturity.

Rising to the Challenge

Just as college demands more from your writing, college professors expect more from you as an individual. While high school teachers may have been lenient if you missed deadlines, or repeatedly nagged you to complete your work on time, college professors expect you to conduct yourself professionally, like an adult. This means *you* have to examine and cultivate your own mature learning habits. Shirking this responsibility with a series of excuses—indeed, anything less than your best work—will result in a low or failing grade (the same high standards by which the professional world will judge you).

Even when a professor shows you leniency—such as granting you an extension on an assignment—it costs you something valuable. Whether you realize it or not, your failure to meet expectations results in diminished respect, less willingness to help you, and poorer letters of recommendation. In college, respect must be *earned*.

If you wish to earn this respect—as you should—then you must complete your work *correctly*, *on time*, and *to the best of your ability*. You must also accept that you are learning advanced skills in a college environment, with no guarantee of earning A's or B's (these grades are for excellent, not average work). If your grades are lower than expected, your first impulse should not be to accuse your professor of unfairness. Mature students are *proactive*: they seek the professor's feedback to find out *why* they received a particular grade and *how* they can improve future work. Even then, improvement may come slowly and with additional setbacks. That is the nature of learning any art—especially one as complex as writing. There are no shortcuts to serious mastery.

Beyond the Grade

Grades perform only a basic "score-keeping" function. They help to make students aware of how successfully their work meets national and local standards, but they have very little diagnostic value. In other words, grades reveal practically nothing about *why* the student is succeeding or failing, *what* specifically is strong or weak about the student's work, or *how much* progress the student is making on particular skills.

More importantly, grades do *not* measure a student's "potential" or "ability"; they only measure *the quality of what the student produces at a fixed moment in time.* This is one reason why a student who considers herself to be an "A student" may still write a B, C, D, or F paper. Students do not always produce work that represents what they are *capable* of producing. Stress, anxiety, procrastination, time constraints, a heavy workload, reluctance to revise, and other common issues can—and usually do—prevent students from working to their full potential. This is why some professors tell students "not to take grades personally." Although useful as a general measure of progress, a grade is *not* a definitive statement about what you are (or are not) *capable* of achieving.

Confusing matters more, grades are not necessarily accurate measures of progress. From the broad view of a student's academic record—over the course of several semesters—grades may reliably indicate *general* strengths or weaknesses in a student's abilities, but on a case-by-case basis, individual grades can be deceptive. One vital realization in this regard is that **students who are genuinely engaged in learning often see their grades go *down* initially, even though their skills are *expanding* and *improving*.** This is because, in order to learn new skills, students must move outside of their educational "comfort zone": the familiar repertoire of skills and methods they have relied on in the past to succeed. As they venture into unfamiliar territory and experiment with new skills, students will undoubtedly make new mistakes or implement new skills awkwardly. But this is a natural, necessary growth process.

Unfortunately, too many students attempt a new skill, see their grades decline, and immediately resort to older, more familiar methods that worked more successfully in the past. In this way, their unhealthy preoccupation with grades becomes a serious obstacle to education by scaring them away from experimenting with new skills. Unless this attitude is corrected, they will never achieve a higher level of mastery in writing. Writing is an art, and like most arts, it involves a messy learning process of trial-and-error. If you wish to make progress, you must be willing to make mistakes, to ignore some of the setbacks that come with them (including lower grades), and to practice diligently (and repeatedly) until you finally acquire a higher level of mastery.

Practice Makes Perfect

Writing has always been difficult to master, but modern society has made it more difficult than ever. Compared to previous generations, you encounter fewer examples of well-crafted writing in your daily life, perceive a greater disconnect between professional and peer culture, devote less leisure time to reading, get more of your information from watered-down "digest" sources like RSS feeds, and apply less craft in your daily writing activities, such as e-mail or blogging. In short, you receive far less *practice*; or rather, you have more ways to avoid it.

Practice is a difficult concept to convey because competing concepts—such as efficiency and instant gratification—are valued more highly in our modern, technology-obsessed society. As a result, few people of "the digital generation" appreciate how much repetition must be involved in the kind of practice that begets real improvement. Imagine what would happen if you joined a basketball team with a coach who only forced you to "practice" your jump shot *once*. Would you be ready to win on game day? Of course not. To actually benefit from practice, you must repeat each skill thousands of times. That is why coaches run "drills" requiring you to perform the same action over and over and over—until it is so "drilled" into your mind that it becomes second nature: a gesture based more on reflex and instinct than on conscious thought. Only then do you begin to truly possess that skill, and you must *keep* practicing to refine and maintain it.

The same applies to writing. Unfortunately, technology makes it temptingly easy for us to *avoid* a tremendous amount of practice that previous generations could not avoid. Consider the computer, for example. Although word processors are far more convenient than the type writers they replaced, they deprive you of practice. Every time you cut-and-paste a lengthy quotation, you think you're being efficient (and technically, you are), but you're also depriving yourself of *practice*. If you re-type the text word-by-word it may feel tedious, but something very important happens: your brain absorbs each word and relays it through your fingers to the keyboard. The result is a much closer and more immersive encounter with the language of the quoted text. The difference may seem trivial, but re-typing the words *manually* (instead of cutting and pasting) forces you to read the text much more closely and deliberately, allowing your brain to absorb some of the structure, diction, vocabulary, and rhythm of the text you are quoting.

Doing this once will make little difference to your writing, but if you invest this level of effort over your lifetime—every time you quote a text—it can yield tremendous benefits: permitting you to absorb, imitate, and eventually create patterns of language which contain the sophisticated style, tone, and rhythm of a confident, experienced writer. That is precisely why, centuries ago, students practiced copying long sections of famous essays and speeches, word for word: Not to do meaningless "busy work," but to learn, by duplication, how well-composed writing looks, sounds, and flows. The effect is much like listening to music: When you listen to a song repeatedly, you eventually absorb its melody and lyrics; but when you sing along with the song—word for word, note for note— you absorb it considerably faster. Practicing imitating other writers is an excellent way to "tune your ear" to the music of beautifully-composed words. But technology has made it easier for your generation to ignore the details of writing, and that is one significant reason that you may have trouble believing that writing can ever sing like music. Believe me, it can.

Reading Is Practice

The easiest way to "tune your ear" to beautiful writing is to *read*. This advice may disappoint you, since an increasing number of students loathe reading. If you're among those students, you are clinging to an attitude that will seriously hold you back in life. In fact, your distaste for reading has probably already cost you more than you realize. In his book *The Dumbest Generation*, Mark Bauerlein explains that "those who acquire reading skills in childhood read and learn later in life at a faster pace than those who do not. They have a larger vocabulary, which means that they don't stumble with more difficult texts, and they recognize better the pacing of stories and the forms of arguments, an aptitude that doesn't develop as effectively through other media" (59).

Simply put, reading cultivates your intellect. The more you read, the sharper your mind becomes, enabling you to absorb information faster, easier, and better—in every subject, not just literature. More than any other activity, reading trains you to organize and expand your thoughts, to give precise expression to sophisticated ideas, to develop your capacity for logical reasoning, and to appreciate alternative perspectives. But the frequency and consistency with which you read are directly proportionate to the benefits you receive. Bauerlein compares it to exercise: "Go to the gym three times a week and the sessions are invigorating. Go to the gym three times a month and they're painful" (59).

Students think they are making life *easier* by skimming a story or relying on shortcuts like SparkNotes, but they are actually making every other aspect of their education *harder*. In the short term, they may get by with less reading, but over the long term, they deprive themselves of the opportunity to absorb the precise vocabulary, elegant transitions, vivid metaphors, polite qualifications or concessions, and other fine elements of thought and expression that would empower them to cultivate a formidable personal voice. When you read, you aren't just working through a text; you are also exercising and expanding your intellect in valuable ways. When you skip reading *Moby Dick* or *Hamlet*, for example, you aren't just cheating yourself out of a great story; you're depriving yourself of the *power* that comes from having Melville's or Shakespeare's eloquence at your command.

From Crisis to Opportunity

Despite their incomparable importance, literacy skills (reading, writing, analysis, and argumentation) are considered by most students to be dull and unimportant. Regrettably, this decline in interest among students has colluded with a corresponding decline in the quality of our educational system—largely due to the erosion of academic standards—to produce alarming deficiencies by the time students reach the college level.

National statistics now show that a majority of high school graduates are poorly prepared to succeed in college because high school standards are disturbingly low. In its September 2008 report, "Diploma to Nowhere," the Strong American Schools association explained:

> [H]igh school is not rigorous enough. Educators don't demand enough from our students. They often give high marks to mediocre work. Our poll found that most students in college remediation [i.e., learning support] earned As and Bs in high school, with nearly four out of five students listing a grade point average of 3.0 or higher. Almost 60 percent of the students in our survey said that their high school classes were easy. Half said they were bored most or almost all of the time.
>
> Students want more demanding coursework. After enrolling in college, they understand that there are large gaps in their knowledge and skills, and nearly half would have preferred that their high school classes had been more difficult in order to better prepare them for university-level academics….
>
> There is a severe disconnect between the knowledge and skills that students learn in high school and the knowledge and skills they need to succeed in college. (8)

These findings attest to a national crisis in education, but for you, they may also present a wonderful opportunity. In an environment in which everyone else is declining in reading and writing ability, your personal efforts to reverse this trend—to hone your intellectual and expressive abilities—will be more impressive and more valuable than ever before.

If you invest the necessary effort to acquire these skills, you *will* stand out from the crowd of seemingly-qualified job applicants, friends, and romantic partners with whom you may be competing. As a result, the quality of your professional, social, and personal life will improve, as will your confidence and happiness. The work isn't easy, but if you apply yourself diligently, your efforts will be well-rewarded.

Are you ready to begin? Then keep reading.

Professionalism

One dismaying trend in the college environment is the sharp decline in basic professionalism. Students tend to treat college as an extension of the earlier educational culture they inhabited as minors, before they became legal adults. However, since colleges exist to serve *adults* who wish to cultivate mature perspectives and to *professionalize*, professors need to enforce *professional* standards that earlier education neglects. That is why the best professors do not tolerate lazy, irresponsible habits that might seem normal in high school. If you wish to thrive in college, learn to be professional.

Ignoring the rules of professionalism may not always directly harm your grade, but it will cost you something valuable by making professors feel *less* motivated to help you, *less* inclined to believe you when doubts about your integrity arise, and *less* willing to show you leniency (such as a deadline extension) even when circumstances might allow it. Worse, it makes professors reluctant to endorse your character with a strong letter of recommendation, which can cost you a scholarship or a job. Respect—and the supportiveness it brings—must be *earned*.

Another good reason to adhere to professionalism is because education is most effective when you practice disciplined study habits, which neatly coincide with the rules of professionalism in college. Therefore, besides earning greater respect from professors, these habits will help you participate more productively in class, enjoy class more, learn more, and produce better work.

Below are several specific recommendations for students enrolled in a literature or writing-intensive course. Following these habits will improve your studies, as well as make you appear professional and serious about the course.

- **Read the introductions**
  If you skip the critical introductions in your anthology or text, you're cheating yourself of a wonderful resource. Introductions offer a quick, efficient overview of critical issues to consider as you read. That's their purpose: to *save* you work. Read them. You'll find it easier to understand the text, participate in discussion, and identify essay topics.

- **Take notes in the margins of your book**
  Reading for class is more *active* than pleasure reading. Keep a pencil on hand and use the margins to write down questions or ideas that occur to you as you read. Your notes should be short, but clear: just enough to reconstruct your thought process when you review later. Before each class (and before you choose an essay topic), *use* your margin notes to refresh your memory. You will be a keener reader and better contributor to discussion.

- **Speak up in class**
  If you're not involving yourself in class discussion, you're making the course duller and harder for yourself. Clever students use class time to identify paper topics, develop their ideas, locate textual evidence, and identify likely objections. You can steer the discussion toward your interests by posing a thoughtful question or comment, and your peers' responses will help you refine your ideas more efficiently than you could do alone.

- **Review and process what you learn in each class**
  When you leave class discussion, sit down *soon after* to think through the new ideas in your brain. Don't let them be pushed aside and forgotten. The best time to generate paper topics, construct thesis statements, and develop insightful analyses is when your brain is still "turned on" from class discussion. It is also a good time to conduct library research.

- **Use the assignment sheets as tools**
  My assignment sheets are detailed for a reason: They include tips and questions to help guide you through the assignment. Re-read the assignment sheet carefully immediately *before* beginning an assignment. Then read it again *after* you finish your paper to ensure you've satisfied all of the assigned criteria.

- **Research on scholarly databases, not the public Internet or SparkNotes**
  If you struggle to understand a text or a particular issue, use library tools to find *published*, *peer-reviewed* answers to your questions. This material will expand your knowledge and can be credibly incorporated into a formal paper later, saving you time. It will also impress your professor and avoid the creativity-killing effect that results when you read abbreviated or simplified notes and summaries on the public Internet.

- **Begin assignments well in advance of the due date**
  Forming a good idea takes time. Developing that idea takes even longer. If you wait until the last minute, you aren't seriously trying to reach your full potential. Your best work is only achieved when you revise and refine your ideas through multiple drafts, as well as workshop those drafts with trained readers. Start your assignments early, *at least* a full week in advance; otherwise, you're hindering your own development.

- **Use the "Writing Effective Essays" guide and the Writing Center**
  This guide will assist you as you write and can be used as a final checklist for competent writing. Before you turn in a paper, check it against this guide's recommendations and lists of common mistakes. Since writing is a form of communication, you should also test the clarity of your ideas on a real audience. Visit the Writing Center multiple times to work with a dedicated tutor who is trained to offer constructive feedback.

- **Read your essay aloud**
  The surest way to detect problems with the flow and structure of your writing is to read it aloud. Your ear will catch mistakes that your eye overlooks. Keep revising until you can read through smoothly without stumbling over awkward sentences and ideas.

- **Format your essay properly**
  Improper formatting conveys a poor impression about your work ethic and encourages the reader not to take your ideas seriously. It may even seem discourteous or insulting to your professor. Follow the rules in the *Formatting* section to ensure that your work looks credible.

- **Read and reflect on professor feedback**
  When you receive feedback, consider it carefully and plan out strategies to improve for the next assignment. Also, be proactive: schedule time to meet with your professor for a thorough discussion of the quality of your work. Do *not* wait until late in the semester to do this because it will likely be too late. If you genuinely want help, seek it early so you can make use of the feedback you receive.

The Golden Rule: Clarity

Of all the rules and guidelines that apply to academic writing, there is one rule that trumps all others: **Writing must be clear.**

Clarity means more than choosing words the reader understands. It means stringing those words together in smooth, coherent sentences; braiding those sentences into logical, flowing paragraphs; and weaving those paragraphs together to explain and develop a central, unifying claim. Clear writing leads the reader through your entire thought process in a precise and compelling manner.

Clear expression requires precise word choice. In verbal communication, poor language skills may be compensated by nonverbal cues, such as facial expressions and tone of voice. Since writing lacks these nonverbal cues, language deficiencies become much more obvious. An imprecise vocabulary no longer suffices. You must choose words carefully to convey the delicate distinctions, subtle movements of thought or logic, and fine shades of meaning which comprise a clear message.

Clear expression *is* sophisticated; dense or "fancy" language is not. Formal writing doesn't need an inflated vocabulary to sound intelligent. Avoid using a thesaurus to replace familiar words with more grandiose terms. Good writing is clear and precise, not dense or fancy. Stick to familiar terms, and only use denser words when they genuinely improve the precision of your message.

Clear expression is learned through trial and error. You must keep drafting and revising in order to master the art of writing. Improvement takes time and practice. You will never fully master clear expression because many concepts (love, happiness, goodness, etc.) exceed the expressive capacity of human language. But you will *improve* at expressing yourself in ways that yield substantial rewards if you seek feedback from others and reflect on your writing often.

Consider this sentence from a student essay about Poe's "The Cask of Amontillado":

> In the beginning of the story, the author showed symbolism by the words he used.

This sentence is profoundly unclear. One problem is the lack of precision: Technically, authors don't "show symbolism"; they *use* symbolism to show or symbolize something *else*. Be precise.

Another problem is the lack of specificity: It is impossible to know what *kind* of symbolism the student is referring to. A more descriptive phrase such as "death imagery" or "the dreary mood of the catacombs" would help, but more clarification might be needed. Be specific.

Furthermore, the student expresses interest in the author's diction ("the words he used"), but does not indicate *which* words, or what *kinds* of words, are significant. If there are too many to list, characterize them generally or refocus the sentence on their effect on readers. Be thorough.

In its present form, the sentence conveys only the absurdly obvious point that authors use words to convey meaning. Despite its grammatical correctness, the sentence communicates nothing meaningful. I'm certain the student has a clearer, more interesting idea *in mind*, but that idea is not making it *onto the page*. Thus, the writing is unclear.

Literary Analysis

Literary analysis (or "interpretation") occurs when you offer a *plausible* and *productive* opinion about what a text "means" on a deeper level than the obvious actions and events of the plot.

A **plausible** opinion can be supported with textual evidence to show that it fits the text in a fair, reasonable manner. The evidence reassures readers that you are not forcing or "projecting" a set of values or meanings onto a text that does not actually bear them.

A **productive** opinion teaches readers something about the text they would not necessarily or readily recognize on their own. It helps them appreciate the text in a deeper, fuller, more insightful way, prompting them to reconsider or refine their own opinions about the text.

Summary vs. Analysis

Summary restates what happens in a text by repeating the plot and obvious surface details. Analysis makes *reasoned claims* about *how* and *why* the text *matters* or *conveys meaning* by interpreting the text's form, characters, situations, or details in ways that are not obvious.

For example, if we **summarize** *Cinderella*, we would retell the events that occur:

> Cinderella is a young lady who lives in poverty, suffers mistreatment from her stepmother and stepsisters, receives help from a fairy godmother, visits a royal ball in a magic dress and carriage, wins the prince's heart, runs away at midnight when the spell ends, returns to poverty, and is finally rescued when a glass slipper reveals her to be the woman the prince loves.

Anyone who reads *Cinderella* should already know these details because they are obvious plot elements. If we **analyze** *Cinderella*, however, we might form this interpretation:

> The story of *Cinderella* reveals that people who live in poverty fail to thrive in society only because they lack socially-acceptable attire and reliable transportation. Yet when such accoutrements are provided to them, they excel at the same activities as the upper classes, and their true dignity and worth shine through. The story exposes the injustice and artificiality of divisions based on class, wealth, or lineage by demonstrating that poor individuals like Cinderella are fully capable of upward mobility. Only their lack of means and the cruelty of the middle classes—symbolized by the stepmother and stepsisters—holds them down.

This is what *Cinderella* could mean on a deeper level. These insights should help others understand the story in a different, more thoughtful way, which confirms that this interpretation is *productive*.

To show that this interpretation is also *plausible*, we might explain that, as an unpaid laborer in rags, Cinderella represents the poor, while her better-dressed step-relatives represent the middle class and the prince represents the upper class. The fairy godmother's "magic" transforms Cinderella outwardly by providing her with clothes and a carriage to attend the ball, but it does not change her inwardly. Since the prince's love persists even after her return to poverty, it appears to be her her innate worth, not her magic clothes which capture his heart. In short, this interpretation makes plausible sense, without skewing or contradicting the story's details.

Feed Curiosity, Don't "Fill Pages"

If you approach writing in perfunctory terms, merely trying to "fill pages" instead of asking yourself what you really want to *say* about the text, the writing process will be difficult, tedious, and unrewarding. Without genuine curiosity or conviction, your ideas will be weak and prone to wander off topic, causing the structure and organization of your writing to suffer. From your perspective, you will settle for throwing in whatever "stuff" you can say to fill space, but from your professor's perspective, your paper will lack coherence, development, and conciseness. Worse, it may suggest that you feel apathetic about the coursework, which is *never* a good impression to convey. (Some day you may need a letter of recommendation from your professor. Do you really want to convey a poor work ethic or negativity toward writing?)

The real problem is that it is virtually impossible to produce good writing if you aren't interested in your topic or the texts you are analyzing. If you don't *care* about what you can contribute to the discussion, writing will never feel natural or enjoyable. This is the hardest reality of writing for most students to discover: until you believe that **your thoughts and your voice *matter***, it is virtually impossible to make significant improvements in your writing.

Of course, you can't expect to feel interested in topics automatically or because your professor "makes" you interested. **It takes *work* to build and nurture sincere interest.** Think about that statement for a few moments. Work is a necessary step in building the kind of interest that will sustain clear, focused, well-developed writing, but students typically approach this process backwards. Most will invest hard work at analysis only if the text and topic *already* interests them; very few understand that interest arises only *after* a text or topic has been carefully and diligently explored—partly through close reading, partly through responsible research.

Getting Curious

Rather than waiting until the last minute and worrying about filling pages, start your writing assignments early—*well in advance of the due date*—so you have time to nurture your curiosity and to identify a truly interesting set of questions worth pursuing.

Class discussion is meant to assist you with this initial question-asking process. If you listen for patterns of recurring interests in your professor's and peers' comments, you will be able to identify moments in the text that deserve further thought and discussion. As you begin to identify these moments, **trust your curiosity**. It will lead you to issues you actually *want* to explore further.

Of course, curiosity does not arise by magic. The most important step in learning to enjoy writing and interpretation is to **read carefully so that it is possible to engage meaningfully with the text.** When you read the text closely—asking yourself questions and taking notes about your thoughts—the writing process becomes *enjoyable* instead of painful. You begin to feel *driven* by a genuine desire to answer fascinating questions, rather than burdened with the tedious task of filling pages with hollow or strained ideas dressed up in clever language. If the latter experience sounds familiar to you, it means you haven't learned how to read with enough attentiveness.

As you dig into the text, you should also **meet with your professor** to discuss your ideas. This will help ensure that your thoughts about the text are taking shape in a manner appropriate for literary analysis. Often, students approach texts in ways that are not proper for literary analysis, but if they don't seek their professor's feedback early on, they may not discover the problem until after the assignment has been submitted for grading—when it is too late to fix. Don't risk it. Seek guidance early on.

There is another reason to visit your professor early on. Most students don't visit office hours until very late in the semester, when they usually show up to ask about "extra credit" to raise their grade. This is very frustrating because even if the professor is willing to offer extra credit, it creates more work for all involved—and for foolish reasons. Students who have the maturity to start their assignments *in advance* and to consult regularly with their professor don't need extra credit. They succeed without extra credit because their "extra" effort is applied where it rightfully belongs: to the existing assignments. They also benefit from hearing their professor's feedback *before* the paper is submitted for grading.

Identifying a Topic

A "paper-worthy" topic is an idea about the text which is insightful, productive, and can be adequately supported and developed within the assigned page range.

Virtually any observable aspect of a text can become the basis for a strong interpretive claim. It could be something that pervades the story—the setting, the society, the plot—or a small detail such as a character's nickname, a recurring color, or a prominent item like a porcelain doll or a broken clock. It could be an aspect of characterization, such as a significant belief, emotion, or personality flaw. It could be a particular technique used by the author, such as distorted chronology, omitted information, or shifting perspectives. It could be the literary form—sonnet, ode, tragedy, or comedy—or a stylistic feature such as blank verse or sprung rhythm. What matters is that you must be able to form a claim that is *not obvious* and *meaningfully enriches our understanding of the text*.

The best places to find topics are in your notes, in class discussion, and through library research.

Notes and Brainstorming

For every literary text you read, write down a few significant questions or ideas that you have about the text. Alternatively, keep track of your answers to these two questions:

- What events, decisions, scenes, or details in the text puzzle you most, and why?

- What is the main theme or "message" of the text? What do you think the author wants us to learn from this story?

If you keep track of puzzling moments and major themes in everything you read, it will be much easier to identify interesting questions for analysis and to form productive connections between texts. Unfortunately, too many students neglect note-taking. Without notes to help organize and clarify their thoughts about literature, these students face unnecessary stress and extra work when it comes time to choose a paper topic and to develop a strong thesis.

Another good approach is to begin by thinking about main characters. Get a sheet of scratch paper, write down the characters' names, and list their defining characteristics. Include basic information like gender, age, and occupation (if known), but also try to describe their personalities, their values, attitudes, talents, and flaws. Often, characters represent certain types of people in society, so as you think about these characters, consider what positive or negative characteristics the author might be praising or critiquing—whether in certain types of people or in human nature as a whole.

Class Discussion

In a literature and writing course, the purpose of class discussion is to help students understand the texts and to engage with them in thoughtful, productive ways. There is rarely time to fully "figure out" a text, but if you pay careful attention and participate in discussion, you will find the task of writing about these texts to be much easier.

Unfortunately, some students never contribute to the discussion, and others settle merely for answering the basic questions their professor asks. There is a tremendous difference between merely offering a few comments that "spring to mind," and sincerely engaging the class with well-considered questions and interests. Think of class discussion as a rare opportunity to test out your ideas on others, and to receive your peers' assistance in developing and refining those ideas. Not only will your papers be better, but you will enjoy class time much more.

Library Research

Too many students think of research as a long process of finding support to "prove" a thesis that they settled upon *before* going to the library. This is backwards. Real research begins with curiosity about an issue, which is then nurtured and developed through responsible research.

Once you identify a topic that interests you, visit the library and start reading articles to find out what others have said about that topic. As you do, pay attention to the ideas *you* wish you could contribute to the discussion: What are these critics *not* saying? What are they overlooking? What are they misunderstanding about the text? Asking (and answering) questions like these will help you identify the *contribution* that your own research paper can make to the discussion. This ensures that the ideas in your paper will be *relevant*, which is vital to a successful paper.

Formulating a Question

Most students find it easiest to select a topic by identifying an interesting question about a literary text. The question can focus on a particularly puzzling moment, a prominent quote, or a seemingly-significant detail in the story that you wish to explore further.

Here are three sample topics that pose an interesting question about three popular short stories:

Nathaniel Hawthorne, "Young Goodman Brown"
At the devilish assembly in the woods, Hawthorne describes the dark baptism by which the worshippers become "partakers of the mystery of sin, more conscious of the secret guilt of others, both in deed and thought, than they could now be of their own" (89). Contemplate this idea carefully. What exactly is the "mystery of sin" as it is here described? How might this description help us to understand the nature of Young Goodman Brown's despair and his gloomy end?

Joyce Carol Oates, "Where Are You Going, Where Have You Been?"
In this story, the impulsive Connie and predatory Arnold Friend both appear to be living a "carpe diem" lifestyle because both characters seem preoccupied with pleasure, excitement, and thrill-seeking. If we suppose, for the moment, that Oates wrote the story as a *commentary* on the young, impulsive values that comprise the "carpe diem" mentality, what might Oates be saying about the "carpe diem" lifestyle? What does she consider dangerous about "carpe diem" thinking and why?

Flannery O'Connor, "Good Country People"

O'Connor writes that Joy-Hulga "took care of it [her leg] as someone else would his soul" (112). But Joy-Hulga is an avowed atheist whose leg is stolen by another atheist (Manley) disguised as a bible salesman. The only "religious" people in the story are uneducated folks like Mrs. Hopewell and Mrs. Freeman. What is O'Connor suggesting about the relationship among religion, education, and morality? Is education or religion more conducive to a moral society, and why?

Each of these samples asks a specific question about a significant or puzzling detail in the story. This helps the writer focus on solving a particular interpretive problem, and makes it much easier to write a strong, focused, insightful paper. Of course, you have to begin with a question that is worth pursuing and appropriate for literary analysis, which your professor can help with.

Inserting Your Voice

As you choose a topic, you should also consider how to *strategize* your approach to maximize your opportunities to contribute fresh and creative insight.

For example, when analyzing a text by a famous author (i.e., any widely-discussed "classic," such as "Young Goodman Brown" or *Moby Dick*), it can feel impossible to contribute something "unique" that critics haven't already addressed. One elegant solution is to formulate your topic as a *comparative analysis*, in which you compare and contrast *two* texts. Even if both texts are well known, situating them in dialogue to consider whether they agree or disagree about an issue can create considerable room for new insights. An astonishing number of critics have written about Shakespeare's *Othello*. Many have also written about Edgar Allen Poe's "The Cask of Amontillado." But only a tiny fraction of critics have compared and contrasted *Othello* with "The Cask of Amontillado" to determine what Shakespeare and Poe are each suggesting about the nature of betrayal.

When you take the comparative analysis approach, the key is to resist the urge to choose two texts that *immediately* seem easy to compare. Often, it is more enjoyable and productive to select two texts that seem to have *very little in common*, then to explore them closely for common themes, situations, characters, or structural and stylistic elements. This approach won't always work, but it often leads to unlikely comparisons between texts that yield very creative and illuminating results.

If comparative analysis is out of the question, another good strategy is to start with the text you find most "interesting" and immediately dive into the research process, *without* formulating a thesis. Think about the main issues that arise in the text, use those terms to search for scholarly criticism, and start skimming or reading until you find a critic you *strongly disagree with*. Disagreement is an excellent spur to writing. Most students find it much easier to formulate a thesis and sustain a coherent, developed argument when writing in *response* to a source the student wishes to refute. The only significant risk involved with this approach is that you may become so focused on responding to one source that it becomes difficult to bring other voices into the discussion.

Yet another productive approach is to second-guess your own initial assumptions about a text. This works particularly well for texts that contain seemingly unnecessary or strange episodes, such as one of the seemingly-digressive subplots in a Shakespeare play or a character who disappears abruptly from a narrative like the Dwarf in Book One of Spenser's *The Faerie Queene*. Rather than dismissing these oddities as "pointless" or "weird," *force* yourself to think seriously about their purpose. Assume that the strange material is *vitally important* to the text in some way, then try your best to discover and explain its purpose. This can be a fun approach—a lot like solving a puzzle—and it frequently leads to useful readings of scenes, events, or characters that most readers ignore or trivialize. That means there should be plenty of room for you to make an insightful contribution.

Introduction

A good introduction gets straight to the point. A great introduction also engages your reader's interest. Every introduction should perform three tasks:

1. **identify an appropriate topic**
   An appropriate essay topic is a specific issue, concern, or question with a clearly defined *scope* and obvious *relevance to the text*.

   Generic concerns such as "race," "gender," "religion," or "patriotism" are *not* appropriate essay topics because they lack scope and relevance to the text. They become essay topics when you specify scope and relevance: "how the author challenges racial assumptions"; "why gender stereotypes create tensions between two main characters"; "how the text exposes religious hypocrisy"; "why the author equates patriotism with cowardice." These are essay topics. Notice that each begins with the word "how" or "why".

2. **explain why the topic merits consideration**
   There are many ways to indicate why your topic is worthy of consideration: (1) identify a serious misperception you intend to correct; (2) identify an issue commentators consistently ignore; (3) indicate why your argument is more productive or plausible than others; (4) explain why a prevailing view must be qualified or expanded in light of new evidence; or (5) explain how your argument changes the way readers understand the broader themes and meaning of the text.

3. **state your central argument (thesis)**
   The thesis is a concise, one-sentence statement of the main argument that you will develop and support in the body of the essay. In academic writing, it is the last sentence of the introduction.

As the list above suggests, a successful introduction answers three important questions:

1. What is the specific topic that your paper will discuss?

2. Why is this topic worthy of discussion and important to the text(s) you are analyzing?

3. What is the *specific* argument you will illustrate and defend?

The reader should not need to read beyond your introduction to find out *what* you will argue or why it *matters* to how we understand the literary text(s) being analyzed. The only reason readers should need to read further is for a detailed explanation of *how* and *why* your argument is supported by the text(s) and adds meaningfully to our understanding.

Many students know that the introduction should begin with a general statement that becomes increasingly specific as the paragraph leads into the thesis. Technically, this is true, but most students misunderstand this model. Often, they begin with absurdly *vague* or *cosmic* statements about "human history" or "the beginning of time," which immediately sabotages the clarity and force of the introduction. Never waste the reader's time with broad issues that do not directly relate to the text(s) you will analyze. Even a "general" introductory statement should get directly to the point, communicating the topic as specifically as possible.

Common Mistakes: Introductions

These common errors always spoil an introduction:

- **Cosmic openings**: Since the beginning of time, man has faced disease and death. One deadly disease is cancer. Cancer afflicts the main character of the play *Wit*.

  None of this is remotely interesting. It is too generic to be helpful. Get to the point.

- **Broad generalizations**: The Renaissance was a time of great tumult. During this period, Catholic corruption spurred the Protestant Reformation, England broke from papal authority, a woman sat on the throne, and political tensions led to a civil war that ended with the beheading of a king. Views about gender, politics, religion, science, authority, and individuality were changing rapidly.

  None of this is literary analysis and it oversimplifies in ways that may annoy well-informed readers. Some topics need brief historical contextualization, but avoid sweeping generalizations that delay the *literary* topic and texts. Get to the point.

- **Generic meta-analysis**: When reading George Orwell's story "Shooting an Elephant," one can speculate and conclude many ideas and thoughts about the interpretation of this story. In fact, many of the critical theories share as many similarities as they do oppose each other with major differences.

  These claims are so generic that they communicate *nothing* meaningful—not even a clear sense of a topic. Get to the point.

- **Dictionary definitions**: Postpartum depression is defined as "depression following the birth of a child, when the mother feels overwhelmed by the child's needs." This disorder probably affects the narrator of "The Yellow Wallpaper" because she has a child and is depressed.

  Defining unfamiliar terms is important in an essay, but it rarely makes a good opening. Usually, it sounds flat, dull, or pedantic. Find a more engaging way to begin.

- **Failure to identify the author(s) and text(s)**: What is most remarkable about the presentation of race in this novel is how little the author appears interested in discussing it. Indeed, the author's language becomes evasive during the novel's most racially-charged moments.

  The reader will wonder: *Which* novel? *Which* author? The introduction must identify the author(s) and text(s) you will discuss, or the reader will be confused.

- **References to the assignment or the preliminary research process**: When assigned to write an essay about *Macbeth*, I was inspired to do research about witches. I never knew there were so many books about witchcraft! I think this is an excellent essay topic!

  This information serves no purpose. It delays any sign of actual analysis. Get to the point.

- **References to class discussion**: After our discussion of Robert Olen Butler's story "Jealous Husband Returns in Form of Parrot," I think more should be said about Bob's idea that the narrator is delusional.

  Referring to what happened "in class" automatically alienates any reader who is not in your class. Your writing should feel accessible even to those who weren't in class. Find a better way to introduce the topic.

Thesis

The thesis is the single most important component of an analytical essay. It concisely states exactly what you will argue in the essay. It also establishes the scope and organization of the body.

In literary interpretation, a strong thesis satisfies three criteria:

- **it advances a *claim*, not merely an observation**
An observation merely states that something happens or is observable in the text, such as: "Bathsheba Everdene falls in love with Gabriel Oak." A *claim* interprets or explains that observation: "Bathsheba Everdene falls in love with Gabriel Oak because he is the only suitor who treats her as an equal." The best claims also clarify how they *matter* to our understanding of the broader purpose or meaning of the text. For example: "By showing how Gabriel Oak's loyalty and respect finally earn Bathsheba Everdene's love, Hardy demonstrates that friendship is more valuable and essential to human happiness than the romanticized passions represented by Frank Troy."

- **the claim is *reasonable* and *demonstrable***
A claim is reasonable if another person can reasonably disagree with it, and it is demonstrable if it can be supported with textual evidence. "Iago turns Othello's own jealousy against him" is not reasonable because no one could reasonably deny that Iago exploits Othello's jealousy. Likewise, "Shakespeare originally intended the play Othello to be a comedy" is not demonstrable because there is no available evidence.

- **the claim contributes *meaningfully* to our understanding of the text**
No one expects you to pose a claim that has never been considered before. However, your claim should contribute productively to critical discussion. It is not sufficient to repeat what others have already said, either in print or in class. Your thesis must correct, qualify, refute, or elaborate upon existing views in an *insightful, productive* manner.

In formal analysis, the thesis is the last sentence of the introduction. It should be expressed in strong, direct, clear terms. A successful thesis tells your reader exactly what you believe and (briefly) why it merits consideration. The only reason readers should need to read further is to find out *why* and *how* your argument is supported by, and affords productive insight into, the text.

Common Mistakes: Theses

Here are some typical errors that make for very poor thesis statements:

- **Delayed or evasive claims:** In this essay, I will discuss whether or not Arnold Friend is a real person and why it matters to Oates's story.

  This announces what you "will" do instead of actually *doing* it. A strong thesis *reports the conclusions you have already reached* (and want your reader to reach). It does not keep the reader in suspense, doubt, or confusion. Lay out your claims directly. For example:

  Arnold Friend is a figment of Connie's imagination symbolizing fear and guilt about her sexual promiscuity, as well as the horrific self-loathing that results when her empty relationships are finally laid bare.

- **Generic patterns:** The authors' depictions of hypocrisy in "Young Goodman Brown" and "Good Country People" are similar, yet different.

  Any two things may be "similar but different," so it is pointless to compare texts in such generic terms. The thesis must identify *specific* similarities and differences, explaining why they *matter*. For example:

  Both authors examine the personally- and communally-destructive consequences of hypocrisy, but while Hawthorne believes religious extremists are especially prone to hypocrisy, O'Connor suggests that a far worse kind of hypocrisy lurks within the intellectual atheist.

- **Unexplained observations:** In terms of their religious views, Antonio and Shylock are unexpectedly similar, but in terms of their business practices, they are opposites.

  This observation specifies a similarity (religion) and a difference (business) that may merit consideration, but it fails to make any significant point about that observation. The reader is left wondering: "So what?" The thesis must clarify why and how the observation is *meaningful* and *important* to the text.

- **Vague references to "complex" or "interesting" ideas:** Careful examination of the color green in *The Great Gatsby* shows that F. Scott Fitzgerald's use of imagery is much more complex than it initially seems.

  Merely calling something "complex" or "interesting" does *not* constitute an argument. You need to make a claim about how that complexity *functions* and why it *matters* to how we understand the text.

- **Purely aesthetic judgments:** The numerous ambivalences of Zora Neale Hurston's novel *Their Eyes Were Watching God* confirm that the novel is not fully finished and therefore does not accurately reflect Hurston's views on race.

  It is rarely productive to pursue purely aesthetic claims about a text. The perception that a text is "good" or "bad," "finished" or "incomplete" is profoundly subjective and virtually impossible to prove. Instead, always assume that a text represents the author's best attempt to convey what he or she wished to convey, and that some part of it is worthy of appreciation. If something about the text seems problematic or off-putting, a good place to begin is by asking, "Why might the author have *wanted* the text to seem this way?"

- **Speculative claims:** If the villagers in "The Lottery" were more altruistic and less influenced by the mob mentality, the victims of their murderous acts could have been treated so much better. Or another example: If Macbeth had ignored the witches, he would not have been infected with the murderous ambition that dooms him and would have enjoyed a happier relationship with his wife.

  These claims are *speculative*, not analytical. Instead of speculating about what *could have* happened in the story, your thesis must present a strong claim analyzing what *does* happen and why it is meaningful.

The Body

The "body" of the essay consists of everything except the introduction (first paragraph) and the conclusion (last paragraph). It provides support and explanation for the thesis, and clarifies how your argument contributes productively to a broader critical discussion about the meaning of a text.

To make a formidable impression, the body must reassure the reader that your thesis (1) fits the details of the text in a plausible way, (2) uncovers deeper meaning in the text than would be obvious through casual reading, and (3) corrects, clarifies, or expands on some important aspect of the text which other critics have overlooked, ignored, or misunderstood.

Structurally, the body requires you to make careful use of **transitions** and **topic sentences** to clarify the logic and flow of your thoughts as you present claims in support of your thesis. You also need **evidence** and **development** to clarify, support, and expand on the claims you make.

Understanding Structure

"Structure" refers to the organization and flow of your ideas, or more specifically, the order in which your thoughts unfold and present themselves to the reader, paragraph-by-paragraph, sentence-by-sentence, word-by-word. The order of those elements should never be random or careless. Instead, you must select an order that *allows the reader to follow your thoughts easily* and that *addresses the reader's most likely questions or objections* along the way.

Explaining what structure *is*, or how to construct it well, is difficult. There are many ways to structure an argument successfully, but even small nuances of structure can make or break the clarity of your message. Mastering those nuances takes a lot of time and practice—much more than can be accomplished in a single semester (or two, or three). But if you begin devoting more time and care to the organization and flow of your writing, not just the content, you will greatly improve the clarity and persuasiveness with which your ideas come across.

Clothing: Dressing for Success

Perhaps the best way to understand how structure affects your writing is to compare it to another kind of language in which most people are much better practiced: clothing.

We don't usually think of clothing as a kind of language, but our clothes do convey messages about who we are and what we value. Since we have to dress ourselves every day, we get a lot of practice trying out different "looks" or "styles." This means that most of us develop a fairly sophisticated understanding of the "language of clothing," including how to nuance its messages for different occasions and audiences. For example, most of us know that when a man attends a professional job interview, he should wear a collared shirt, a tie, a belt, and pants—*not* a T-shirt, a baseball cap, a pair of suspenders, and shorts. Since there are particular expectations for proper professional attire, interviewers will evaluate your credibility partly on the basis of how well you dress the part of a professional.

Are these expectations logical? Not really. There is no reason that a man who arrives to an interview in shorts *cannot* be just as intellectually-qualified as a man who arrives in pants; but clothing communicates something important about the man's awareness or willingness to follow professional expectations. Arriving to an interview in a T-shirt and shorts effectively tells the interviewer: "I don't know how to dress professionally," or worse: "I don't care if I get this job, so I didn't bother to dress up." On the other hand, arriving in appropriate business attire sends a very different message: "I understand the rules of professionalism and I care enough about getting this job that I took the time to dress up."

But the language of clothing is much more sophisticated than these basic considerations. You know that a shirt, tie, and pants are important for an interview, but you *also* know—more specifically— that the shirt must be a solid color (or simple, tasteful pattern) and a button-down (not polo) style; otherwise, it will look ridiculous paired with a tie. Likewise, you know that the pants must be a solid, conservative color—black, brown, gray, tan, or khaki—not checkered, striped, brightly colored, or denim.

Here is where it gets really interesting: While a nice shirt, tie, and pants will convey seriousness about getting a job, an elegant three-piece suit will probably make an even better impression. Yet *somehow* you know that wearing a tuxedo—which is even nicer than a three-piece suit—will *not* convey a more positive impression. In fact, it could have the opposite effect, making you appear insane. This is hard to explain since nicer clothing should imply greater seriousness about the job. Yet we all know that, while it is bad to dress "too casually" for an interview, it can be equally disastrous to dress "too formally" (what we call being "overdressed"). A tuxedo is so formal that it may make you seem desperate, and desperation tends to be viewed just as negatively in our culture as sloppiness or disinterest.

Smaller details further nuance your perceived credibility. A professional tie can be almost any color or abstract pattern, but it *cannot* be covered in cartoons or beer logos if you wish to be taken seriously. Moreover, the tie must be carefully paired with a "matching" shirt. If the tie and shirt "clash" or match too closely—such as a red tie paired with a red shirt of exactly the same shade— they will look ridiculous, despite the fact that either item by itself might be appropriate for an interview. Thus, how well you *combine* different articles of clothing together also affects the message you send.

Even on a subtler level, the details affect your perceived credibility. For example, if you wear a clip-on tie, a tie with a poorly constructed knot, or a tie that is a little too short (or too long) for your torso, you may send another unflattering message: "I put on a tie for this interview, but I am not really the kind of person who wears ties. I'm faking it and I don't know what I'm doing."

A professional hiring agent once explained that he considers a tie clip to be reliable evidence that he is dealing with a genuinely professional male job candidate. In his view, only someone who already owns a lot of ties, and who has spent a lot of time in a professional environment, is likely to own a tie clip. Thus, that one, tiny detail may signal the difference between someone who merely knows how to dress well for an interview, and someone who has professionalized enough to already own a business wardrobe and to understand subtle details of formal etiquette.

Writing: Structuring for Success

What we have been discussing all along is *structure*. If individual pieces of clothing are like words, *how you put those words together to achieve different, nuanced effects* is what we mean by "structure." Much like each item of clothing, individual words or phrases convey a particular meaning, but the clarity and persuasiveness of the message also depend heavily on *how you put those words and phrases together*, and *which details you choose to include or omit*.

With this understanding of structure in mind, consider this: A person who dresses very well for a job interview would immediately sabotage his credibility if he were to add a baseball cap to his outfit or forget to wear his socks. Likewise, a very well written paper can be sabotaged by the presence of an irrelevant paragraph—such as an off-topic discussion about a movie, song, or personal experience— or by the absence of some important element like a thesis or a conclusion.

In the student's mind, it may seem unfair when "small" problems like these significantly lower their grade because students tend to think about grading in *quantitative* terms. They don't believe their grade should be lowered "just because of *one* bad paragraph." But they are missing the point. The real problem is that even "one bad paragraph" can ruin the collective effect of an entire paper. It can have a *qualitative* impact that is much bigger than the sum of its parts, and in much the same way that an employer will not look past a baseball cap or missing socks to trust a person's "professionalism" just because *most* of their outfit is appropriate for a professional interview.

Sample Paper: Basic Structural Elements

The following sample student paper has been stripped down to its basic structural elements so that you can see more clearly the organizational strategy the writer uses to explain the thesis.

The first paragraph is a complete, well-written **introduction**. It clearly identifies the topic the paper will focus on (the rape-like violation of a main character in two literary texts) and leads to a concise **thesis** statement, which is colored in **red**. If you compare this sample introduction to the recommendations in the *Introduction* and *Thesis* sections of this writing guide, you will see that the student has followed those recommendations well.

The body of the paper has been removed except for the **major transitions** and **topic sentences** which the student uses to guide the reader's focus throughout the paper. The major transitions are colored in **blue**. Notice how they divide the student's thesis into four smaller claims that work together to make a persuasive case for the thesis as a whole. This strategy neatly divides the body of the paper into four sections, with each section discussing one part of the thesis and supporting it with textual evidence. In order, the body of this paper will show that:

1. Manley and Carol are *deliberately* deceitful

2. their aggression is provoked by their victim's *education* and perceived arrogance

3. Joy-Hulga and John are *undeserving* victims of such abuse, and

4. Joy-Hulga and John feel *so deeply violated* that the abuse is equivalent to "rape."

If you read only the blue statements aloud, you should be able to hear how they all flow together to comprise the fuller argument expressed as the thesis.

Within each of these sections, the student also uses more specific topic sentences, colored in green, to clarify which text and character is being focused on at any given moment. As the author switches his focus from "Good Country People" to *Oleanna* in each section, the topic sentences also clarify the similarities or differences between the two stories. This is accomplished by brief transitional phrases, such as: "A similar pattern holds true in…" or "Like Joy-Hulga…" Elsewhere, it is accomplished in fuller, more sophisticated form, such as when the student writes: "For John, the loss is less tangible, but no less jarring. Whereas Joy-Hulga defines her identity through her prosthetic leg, John's self-esteem depends on…" Either way, these topic sentences ensure that the reader always knows (1) which text and character is being discussed, (2) what supporting claim will be focused on in that paragraph, and (3) how the two texts compare to each other.

The final paragraph is a complete, well-written **conclusion** which re-states the thesis in slightly different language but also clarifies the merit or "payoff" of the paper's analysis. The reader should be left with a clear sense of (1) what he or she has learned and (2) how it matters to his or her understanding of the texts as a whole. The goal here is to leave the reader feeling as if the analysis has led to a fuller, more meaningful understanding of the texts and their comparative merits. The reader should feel as if he or she has really learned something important.

Student Name

ENGL 1102X

Dr. Kisting

April 1, 2011

Rape and Degradation in "Good Country People" and *Oleanna*

Flannery O'Connor's "Good Country People" and David Mamet's *Oleanna* both present antagonists who violate another person so completely that the transgression is akin to rape, causing the victim to feel completely defiled, though no sexual contact may have occurred. In O'Connor's story, Manley Pointer misrepresents himself as a naïve country boy in order to gain the trust of Joy-Hulga Hopewell and ultimately steal her prosthetic limb, an item which is even more valuable to her than her virginity. In Mamet's play these gender roles are reversed to jarring effect, when Carol attacks John's livelihood, his reputation and even his freedom by making false and incendiary accusations about his conduct. In both stories, these deceitful aggressors play upon their victim's superior education in order to deprive them of a cherished possession—whether it be a prosthetic limb or tenure—which is deeply connected to their sense of self-worth. Both O'Connor and Mamet warn that highly-educated persons may unwittingly inspire anger and resentment from those who are less educated, resulting in a hostile retaliation that is so emotionally-invasive and degrading it can only be likened to rape.

Both Manley and Carol deliberately deceive their victims in order to set them up for abuse. In "Good Country People," Manley sets the highly-educated Joy-Hulga up for abuse by... *Discuss Manley's tactics as a deceiver, highlighting the best evidence of his corrupt intentions.*

A similar pattern holds true in *Oleanna*, although here the gender roles are reversed. Carol sets her professor John up for abuse by... *Discuss Carol's tactics as a deceiver, highlighting the best evidence of her corrupt intentions.*

Both Manley and Carol lash out specifically at their victims' superior education, which they seem to resent as a form of arrogance. Although Manley feigns respect for Joy-Hulga's education, he is actually feeding her ego to blind her to his real ulterior motives. *Discuss Manley's pretense of respect for Joy-Hulga's intelligence, and his later retaliation against that intelligence, including his accusation that she "ain't so smart."*

Much like Manley's flattery toward Joy-Hulga, Carol initially pretends to seek John's expertise so that she can understand the material in his course, but she is actually baiting him into making remarks that she can use against him later. *Discuss Carol's pretense of respect for John's intelligence, and her later retaliation against that intelligence, including her accusations that he is "elitist" and arrogant.*

Neither Joy-Hulga nor John deserves the abuse enacted against them. Joy-Hulga may strike many readers as arrogant, however this arrogance is really a defense mechanism designed to conceal her emotional weaknesses and her desire to be loved…. *Discuss Joy-Hulga's character, acknowledging the potentially off-putting aspects of her character, but persuading the reader that she is fundamentally innocent and well-intended in order to show that she does not deserve to be attacked by Manley.*

Like Joy-Hulga, John also strikes some readers as arrogant, however he is clearly more innocent than Carol and makes several gestures that suggest his desire to help…. *Discuss John's character, acknowledging the potentially off-putting aspects of his character, but persuading the reader that he is fundamentally innocent and well-intended in order to show that he does not deserve to be attacked by Carol.*

For both Joy-Hulga and John, the experience of abuse so thoroughly deprives them of their sense of security and self-respect that it is tantamount to rape. In Joy-Hulga's case, we are told that she took care of her prosthetic leg "as someone else would his soul, in private and almost with her own eyes turned away" (112). *Discuss the loss of her leg and the vulnerable moments of trust leading up to that violation, highlighting the traumatic impact that the event has on Joy-Hulga.*

For John, the loss is less tangible, but no less jarring. Whereas Joy-Hulga defines her identity through her prosthetic leg, John's self-esteem depends on his occupation, his impending tenure, and his book—all of which Carol sabotages viciously. *Discuss the loss of his professional credibility, as well as the vulnerable moments of trust leading up to that violation, highlighting the traumatic impact that the event has on John.*

Both O'Connor and Mamet demonstrate that even well-educated people can be deceived and deprived of their dearest possession. Whereas Joy-Hulga loses a false leg that symbolizes her entire sense of self worth, John loses the tenure that would safeguard his future and his family. In both cases, these vital possessions are stripped away so maliciously and degradingly that the violation amounts to a kind of rape. Neither character recognizes the danger until it is too late because their assumption of superior intelligence blinds them to their own vulnerabilities and causes them to underestimate their attackers. The lesson of these works is to be cautious even when one thinks oneself unassailable and to retain a sense of humility in all cases. As O'Connor and Mamet show, education does not guarantee the individual superiority over his or her opponents, and it may even become the target of an attack.

Transitions

Transitions are the glue that holds the paper's structure together. They clarify the flow of logic from one sentence, paragraph, or idea to the next. **In other words**, transitions help readers follow your thoughts, step by step. They may be complete sentences, short phrases, or single words.

If you use transitions poorly—**or worse**, omit them—your readers will feel confused or unconvinced about the connections you try to establish in your analysis. **As a result**, those readers will instinctively resist your claims or even stop reading. **In contrast**, well-crafted transitions grant you surprising *control* over a discussion, allowing you to steer your reader's minds in the direction you choose, toward the conclusions you want them to reach. This is true **not only** in formal writing, **but also** in verbal communication.

In this regard, well-crafted transitions are like a super-power: a kind of subtle mind control that, properly used, will get people thinking only about those things you want them to think about, and nothing that you don't. This is called "focus." Writers with a good sense of focus know how to use precise transitions to *avoid*, *suppress*, or *redirect* an audience's natural tendency to wander off-topic or misunderstand what is being communicated. **Since** this skill is as effective in verbal communication as it is in writing, writers with a good grasp of focus and transitions also tend to be talented at managing people to keep them on task. **Regardless**, your ability to use transitions profoundly affects how others respond to your ideas.

For example, some people will dominate a discussion by constantly interrupting with comments that *force* the other listeners to respond or to leave the discussion. We consider this socially rude behavior **because** the over-assertive speaker "monopolizes" the discussion with his or her own interests and does not allow others to participate equally. **As a result**, the others do not feel that their interests are being heard or respected. **However**, sometimes an exceptional speaker can dominate a discussion—doing most or all of the talking, and focusing exclusively on his or her own interests—*without* irritating you. **If so**, the speaker was probably gifted at using transitions to make his or her interests feel *connected* and *relevant* to your own. **Consequently**, you felt as though you *shared* those interests or believed they were sufficiently *meaningful* and *productive* to deserve your attention. Often, we describe such speakers as "charismatic."

Transition Words

Transitions are powerful, elegant ways to lead a reader from one topic to the next. If you use them well, it is astonishing how successfully you can persuade your reader to follow your thought process and accept your logic. When crafting transitions, it helps to have a suitable vocabulary. I strongly recommend committing the list of words below to memory. These words will help you cultivate precision and control in your writing voice. Look back at the **bold print** in the previous section to see some of these transitions at work. Notice how they "smooth out" the flow of ideas from one sentence or phrase to the next, clarifying the flow of thought.

Words that indicate an *addition, expansion,* or *accumulation* of thought include:

furthermore	in addition	another	equally important
moreover	what is more	so too	more importantly

Words that indicate a *continuation* or *development* of thought include:

so	for this reason	accordingly	the implication is
therefore	because	it follows that	if ... then
consequently	as a result	in this regard	thus

Words that indicate a *departure, change,* or *reversal* of thought include:

on the contrary	however	conversely	nonetheless
on the other hand	alternatively	rather	nevertheless
in contrast	instead	yet	regardless

Words that indicate *connections* and *similarities* among ideas include:

in the same way	likewise	is equivalent to	in the same vein
similarly	just as ... so too	is comparable to	much like

Words that indicate *differences* and *variations* in ideas include:

unlike	contrary to	contrasts with	another approach
in a different way	reverses	differs from	instead

Words that help to clarify *time, sequence,* and *order* include:

earlier	later	currently	meanwhile
previously	first, second, third	subsequently	thereafter
shortly after	next, then	eventually	at length

If, for example, you wish to agree with someone else's idea, but to qualify the extent of your agreement, you could use transition words to clarify your thoughts precisely, like this:

> John Smith is certainly correct that, "in a crisis situation, most people tend to consider their own needs first, before the needs of others" (36); **however**, this does not necessarily prove Smith's subsequent claim that most people are selfish. **On the contrary**, "selfishness" implies an unhealthy obsession with one's own needs, but in a crisis situation, it makes good sense to tend to one's own immediate needs first, before attempting to assist others.

Topic Sentences

A topic sentence is a specific kind of transition. It signals which part of your thesis a specific paragraph (or series of paragraphs) will address by clarifying the specific focus of those paragraphs. It is always important to have strong topic sentences, but especially when a paragraph introduces new ideas that require a logical "leap" from the ideas discussed in previous paragraphs. The topic sentence helps readers make this leap by clarifying your thought process so those readers can follow you coherently.

Imagine that you are writing about Joyce Carol Oates's story "Where Are You Going, Where Have You Been?" and the first paragraph of the body presents textual evidence that Connie's encounter with Arnold Friend is a dream. If the next paragraph *abruptly* starts to discuss the dark side of Connie's sexual fantasies, the reader may get confused. Instead, ease into the second paragraph with a topic sentence that clarifies the flow of logic so that your reader can follow:

> If, in fact, Connie is dreaming [*as the preceding paragraph demonstrated*], then Arnold Friend may be understood as a revealing representation of her subconscious desires and fears with regard to sexual relationships [*as this paragraph will show*].

A topic sentence like this (without the bracketed comments) will successfully link paragraphs together by clarifying the flow of thought. More simply, the topic sentence anticipates and answers the question readers are likely to ask: "What do Connie's sexual fantasies have to do with your earlier claim that Connie is dreaming?" By answering this question, the topic sentence shows how your discussion of one idea leads naturally and logically into the next. Ideally, it also echoes some of the terminology used in your introduction to reassure the reader that you are still on topic and advancing the central thesis.

Development: How and Why?

Development is a relatively abstract concept to most students because daily life rarely requires us to express our thoughts fully or precisely. Most conversations are dominated by trivial concerns we call "small talk" (generic comments about the weather, our health, the weekend, etc.) or by practical requests to obtain something we need or want (information, food, entertainment, etc.). As a result, we are not accustomed to explaining our opinions *at length*, by recounting our *logical reasoning*, the *specific observations* on which such logic depends, or the *precise conclusions* we have reached.

Learning to develop a claim is really about learning to ask productive questions. Generally, it is best to **ask questions that begin with "how" or "why."** Such questions force you to think at the deeper level of *analysis* and *evaluation*, rather than the merely descriptive level of observation or summary. The difference becomes obvious if you apply this rule to questions that arise in daily conversation. While it is easy to answer basic questions of fact, such as "What is your name?," it requires considerably more thought to answer questions like "*How* did you get your name?" or "*Why* did your parents pick that name?" Also, the answers are much more interesting.

The same principle can be applied to literary texts. Asking "how" and "why" questions to encourage deeper, more precise thought about a literary text will dramatically improve quality of your insights.

Consider this claim, written at a basic introductory level for a college essay:

> Frederick Douglass goes to great lengths to portray the perverting effects of slavery on Southern Christianity.

This "claim" is really only a basic observation. It tells us *what* Douglass is doing (or trying to do), but it explains nothing about *how* or *why* Douglass is doing it. Thus, it fails to offer a deeper understanding of Douglass or his narrative. To develop it into a truly insightful and productive analytic claim, we need to ask *how* and *why* questions: (1) *How* does Douglass portray this perversion? (2) *Why* does he consider it important to point out this perversion? (3) *How* does this portrayal serve the narrative's broader goal to encourage the abolition of slavery? And so on.

Asking these questions repeatedly—throughout the entire writing process—will help you articulate deeper, more developed insights about the text. Applied to the example above, you might write:

> Frederick Douglass portrays the perverting effects of slavery on Southern Christianity by showing how cruelty to slaves ingrains itself in the slaveholder's nature and obliterates true Christian morals. Consequently, Douglass demonstrates that slavery is just as detrimental to white slaveholders as it is to black slaves, and suggests that slavery's abolishment is vital not only to the freedom of his own people, but to the salvation of the slaveholder's own soul.

What a remarkable improvement! Compared to the original claim, this version takes us much deeper into *understanding* Douglass's narrative by explaining how and why its structure, content, and presentation *matter* to the meaning readers should take away. This kind of development does not happen overnight. It takes time and multiple drafts, which is why you need to start writing early.

Textual Evidence

There are two kinds of sources in an analytical paper: Primary sources include any texts—poems, plays, short stories, or novels—which serve as the primary *object* of analysis (texts you are analyzing directly). Secondary sources include articles or books that others have written about a literary text in order to debate its meaning or importance (texts engaged in discussion about a primary text).

Quotations and paraphrases from *primary* sources assure your reader that you have read, understood, and analyzed the text carefully—in such a manner that you can competently demonstrate and defend your interpretation using precisely selected details.

Quotations and paraphrases from *secondary* sources assure your reader that you have conducted responsible research about the texts and issues your paper addresses—in such a manner that you can cite and respond productively to what others have said about the same (or related) material.

Primary Sources (Literary Texts)

Use quotations and paraphrases from the primary text to back up every *significant* claim you make. A "significant claim" is any claim that (1) is not plainly evident in the text and (2) another person may reasonably disagree with. Explain each quotation to clarify its relevance to your argument. Cite every quotation using proper parenthetical citation with a corresponding Works Cited page (MLA style).

Inexperienced writers often misuse textual evidence. Whenever you quote or paraphrase the text, you should do all of the following:

- **Quote or paraphrase only as much as is needed to illustrate your point**
  Quotations should read as grammatically correct and coherent statements, but you can use ellipses (…) and square brackets ([ ]) to shrink long quotes, cut out superfluous material, or make minor adjustments to syntax. Lengthy quotations are better handled by paraphrasing the main ideas and selectively quoting only the most important words or phrases

- **Explain what the evidence shows**
  A quote does not necessarily mean the same to your reader as it does to you. Always precede or follow the quote with a clear explanation of what it shows or why it is significant.

- **Clarify the relevance to your thesis or topic sentence**
  You must explain how each piece of evidence relates to your main thesis or a significant supporting argument. Otherwise, the reader may not understand why it is being included.

- **Identify the source with parenthetical citation**
  Readers may wish to find the quoted or paraphrased material in the original text. To assist them, and to credit your sources properly, you must include parenthetical citation.

As these rules suggest, you should never litter your paper with quotations and expect the reader to figure them out or recognize their relevance intuitively. Choose your evidence carefully, explaining what each piece of evidence shows and why it matters. This keeps your argument securely grounded in the text and increases the likelihood you will offer insights the reader may have overlooked.

Consider this sample of well-chosen and properly explained textual evidence, from a paper about Connie and Arnold Friend in the story "Where Are You Going, Where Have You Been?":

> Arnold Friend's sinister sexual intentions gradually come to light when he comes to Connie's house. At first, he reveals information that he should not know: not only Connie's name, but also accurate descriptions of her family and friends. These initial gestures of intimidation and intrusion into Connie's privacy soon give way to more aggressive talk about sexual activity. With obvious sexual implications, Arnold tells her: "I'll come inside you where it's all secret and you'll give in to me and you'll love me" (760). At this moment, his perverse intentions become clear, making Connie feel so overwhelmed that she fails to recognize her own kitchen (761). She is finally beginning to realize the dangerous circumstances her actions have invited, but her severe disorientation strongly suggests that Connie is not equipped to deal with these frighteningly mature consequences of her "adult" flirtations. Predictably, though she resented her parents earlier, she begins to wish for their assistance.

At least four qualities make this passage strong:

- *It prefaces the evidence with topic sentences that clearly signal the paragraph's purpose*: to show how Arnold's "sinister sexual intentions … come to light" and how they affect Connie.

- *It paraphrases unimportant points* (such as Arnold's mysterious knowledge of Connie's family, or Connie's failure to recognize her own kitchen), instead of wasting space on long quotes.

- *It quotes just enough of the text to illustrate important points* (such as Arnold's aggressive statement of sexual desire), instead of quoting whole paragraphs or lengthy dialogue. One well-chosen quote is sufficient to demonstrate Arnold Friend's perverse intentions.

- *It accompanies the quotation with a clear explanation of its significance*. Readers are told that there are "obvious sexual implications" embedded in Arnold's statement, ensuring that they realize it can be read with sexually graphic connotations. They are also reminded how the statement affects Connie, further proving its sexually-intimidating tone.

Together, these qualities add up to a superb use of textual evidence—a good model of the clarity, explanation, and development that you should strive to achieve in your own paper. Of course, getting to this level takes time, effort, and revision.

Explaining Evidence

Often, students fail to explain the evidence they quote, or they provide an explanation that does not clearly relate to what they quoted. Consider this example:

> In "To the Virgins, to Make Much of Time," Herrick says: "The glorious lamp of heaven, the sun,/ The higher he's a-getting,/ The sooner will his race be run,/ And nearer he's to setting" (5-8). With this passage, the author is explaining that when you are young everything is perfect and the more situations seem optimistic, but when you are older those situations turn into fond memories or memorable chances.

The logic of these views is hard to follow because the explanation of Herrick's viewpoint (sentence 2) lacks a clear connection to the lines quoted (sentence 1). Herrick's description of the sun makes no mention of youth, perfection, optimism, or memory, yet all of those ideas show up in the explanation that follows. As a result, the student appears to be forcing an interpretation that does not fit. Perhaps other parts of Herrick's poem do mention youth, perfection, optimism, or memory, but not the lines quoted here.

The solution is to revise the explanation so that it relates clearly to the quote. Here is one possibility:

> In "To the Virgins, to Make Much of Time," Herrick says: "The glorious lamp of heaven, the sun,/ The higher he's a-getting,/ The sooner will his race be run,/ And nearer he's to setting" (5-8). Here, the sun is symbolic of time, which is passing swiftly and will soon come to an end. It also evokes a classic poetic comparison between a person's life and the hours of a day. The sun is still on the rise, which means that the virgins Herrick is addressing are still in the early morning hours of life (youth); however, the sun will soon crest at Noon (metaphorically, middle-age) and begin its decline into evening and darkness (symbolically, old age and death).

This revised explanation is considerably clearer because it now directly echoes the language used in the quotation. Since Herrick specifically mentions the "sun" (and describes its movements), the explanation wisely clarifies that the sun represents *time*, and then unpacks its symbolic relationship to the age of the virgins. They may be in the morning of their youth now, but soon they will have to face the sunset of old age and death.

Secondary Sources (Scholarly Articles)

In a competent research paper, you should cite and discuss *at least five critical sources* which are:

- **credible and scholarly** (published in peer-reviewed books or journals)
- **engaged in *literary* analysis** (making claims about the meaning of a literary text)
    - Note: Do *not* use book reviews, scientific studies, scriptural quotes, or other non-literary, non-analytical sources, *unless approved by your professor*.
- **discussing an author that your paper addresses** (ideally, the same text also)
- **accessed through a library database** (in print or electronically), *not* Google, Yahoo, etc.

In addition to these formal requirements, it is imperative that you choose sources that you consider to be *coherent*, *useful*, and *worthy of discussion*. This does not mean that you should only choose sources that advance an argument you agree with; on the contrary, it is perfectly acceptable to critique and reject another critic's views. However, you must never use sources *superficially* or *dismissively*. You must *engage* each critic in productive discussion.

Never borrow words or ideas from a source without giving proper credit. Failing to credit the source constitutes plagiarism, a very serious form of theft with dire disciplinary consequences. See the *Plagiarism* and *MLA Citation* sections for more information.

Engaging with Criticism

What exactly does it mean to "engage critics in productive discussion"? Basically, it means that you must demonstrate *three important abilities* in your handling secondary sources. You must be able to:

- **identify the critic's argument in clear, relevant terms**
  What exactly does the critic claim and why? How is it relevant to *your* discussion of the text?

- **explain what is useful or problematic about the critic's argument**
  Why is this argument helpful (or what problems does it pose) for understanding the text?

- **clarify your own contribution to the discussion**
  What are *you* contributing that goes beyond what others have already said? Typically, this is revealed in one of three ways:

  - explain why you disagree with the critic's views and offer a corrective view

  - apply the critic's views in a new way or to a different text

  - expand upon the critic's ideas in a productive manner

Common Mistakes: Criticism

Here are some typical errors to avoid when handling critical sources:

- **Giving critics the last word**: Never end a paragraph with a quote or paraphrase from a critic. The end of each paragraph marks the culmination of some supporting part of your thesis, so if you end with what someone *else* has already said, it may look as though you are merely repeating, not enriching, an ongoing discussion. Always follow your secondary sources by explaining how the cited material relates back to *your* argument and *your* ideas.

- **Dismissive responses**: Paul Smith argues that "Connie is unhealthily infatuated with Arnold Friend" (95). That may be, but it is also important to consider Connie's resentment toward her sister June. This student isn't actually responding to the critic. The critic's viewpoint is merely tossed into the mix and then pushed aside dismissively. To legitimately *engage* a critic in discussion, you must respond productively to the ideas presented in the quoted material.

- **Unnecessary block quotations**: Do *not* use block quotations in your paper without your professor's approval. Block quotations waste a lot of space and are *rarely* necessary. Instead, quote selectively. Illustrate your argument with carefully chosen phrases or sentences. If you cannot, then consider paraphrasing the evidence rather than quoting it directly. Block quotations often look like lazy efforts to fill up space, and thus, they tend to weaken a paper.

- **Relying too heavily on a critic**: It is strange and deeply problematic to cite or paraphrase a critic for several paragraphs in a row, or throughout the entirety of a paper. It is best to explain a critic's views once, briefly discuss the merit of those views in relation to your topic, and then move on. If you rely on the same critic for several consecutive paragraphs, or at frequent intervals throughout an entire paper, your reader will begin to doubt that you are contributing fresh insight. It will look as though you are merely repeating another critic. Don't let a critic's viewpoint take over and dominate your paper.

Plagiarism

Plagiarism means using another person's *words* or *ideas* without giving full and accurate credit to the source. Although deliberate plagiarism often leads to more severe penalties—including suspension or expulsion—even accidental plagiarism carries stiff penalties, such as failing the assignment and withdrawal from the course. Either way, you cannot afford to put yourself in that situation.

Since it can be difficult or impossible to prove that plagiarism was an accident, most universities agree that **you are responsible for informing yourself well enough to avoid accidental plagiarism.** Many students are not aware of this rule or do not take it seriously until they are already mired in accusations of plagiarism. Don't be foolish. Take time right now to learn how to cite responsibly.

Penalties

Even the best students may feel tempted to shortcut their way through a heavy workload by copying from unacknowledged sources or purchasing an essay. The temptation is strongest when work from several courses begins to pile up at the end of a semester. Stress and laziness start to work against you, until you may find yourself inventing poor justifications for cheating. But trust me: there is *never* a good reason to plagiarize. The consequences can be dire and irreversible.

If you think that failing the assignment or the course is the worst that can happen, think again. Those are *lesser* penalties often applied to *accidental* plagiarism. If an instructor suspects that the plagiarism may have been intentional, the penalties can be far worse. In ascending order, they are:

- failure of the assignment
- failure of the course
- loss of scholarships and other financial assistance
- suspension from the university
- expulsion from the university
- denial of entrance into ethically-sensitive fields of study (Medicine, Pharmacy, Law, etc.)
- denial of entrance into certain graduate or professional programs
- fines and other civil or criminal penalties

Most universities will not expel you unless you commit two separate instances of plagiarism, but even one instance is serious. Many graduate and professional programs will *not* accept you if there your record contains a case of academic dishonesty. You may also be legally barred from entrance into ethically-sensitive fields, such as those that grant a license to dispense medicine. Scholarships may need to be repaid, career options may disappear, and strong letters of recommendation will be very hard to obtain. In short, one instance of plagiarism can have serious and permanent ramifications for your future—possibly barring you from your personal and professional goals.

Protect Yourself

There are two important rules you should always follow to protect yourself from accidental plagiarism:

- **Identify the source by *name* to credit the source's <u>ideas</u>**
  Whenever you consult a source to obtain information or ideas that you did not already know, you must *identify the source* by the author's name and the page number on which the information appears. If you don't, it will appear to your readers as if *you* are the original thinker who came up with that information; thus, you would be accepting false credit for your source's *thinking effort*.

- **Use *quotation marks* to credit the source's <u>words</u>**
  Whenever you copy a source's exact language—a sentence, a phrase, or any unique term—you must *place quotation marks around the source's words* to show that it was the author, not you, who came up with those words. If you don't, it will appear to your readers as if *you* invested the effort to express the source's ideas into your own well-chosen words; thus, you would be accepting false credit for your source's *writing effort*.

For example, if I were writing a paper about plagiarism, I might quote from a reputable source to explain that plagiarism occurs whenever you "take and use as one's own the thoughts, writings, or inventions of another" (*Oxford English Dictionary*). Here, the quotation marks show exactly which words I copied from my source, while the parenthetical citation identifies the author. Since the *Oxford English Dictionary* is a reference source with many authors, it is sufficient to identify it by title instead. Regardless, I am protected from any risk of plagiarism because I have followed both rules: (1) identifying the source, and (2) using quotation marks to credit the source's words.

Paraphrase

To paraphrase means to *summarize* and *condense*, in *your own words*, an idea derived from another source. However, many students are never taught how to differentiate between *legitimate paraphrasing* and a kind of plagiarism known as *tracing*, which can lead to serious trouble.

Tracing occurs when you alter a source's words and remove the quotation marks, but continue to follow and reproduce (i.e., "trace") the underlying thought process or sequence of ideas. This creates the false impression that *you* authored and sequenced those thoughts, even though that credit properly belongs to the source. Worse, if your professor discovers it, it may appear as though you intentionally plagiarized because the altered wording may look like evidence that you were trying to conceal the theft. Since it is virtually impossible to distinguish conscious from accidental tracing, it hardly matters whether you meant to do it or not.

Whenever you remove the quotation marks and decide to paraphrase a source's ideas in your own words, there are three rules you should always follow:

- The paraphrase must be **significantly shorter** than the source material

- The paraphrase must use **substantially different language** than the source material

- The paraphrase must still **credit the source for the *idea***, in prose or parenthetical citation

If your paraphrase is *not* shorter or *not* in substantially different language, there is no legitimate reason to change the source's words. Paraphrase is intended to save space by condensing and simplifying what someone else has said. If you aren't able to do that, then you should allow the source be heard in his or her own words, through a direct quotation.

Examples

In a published analysis of William Faulkner's "A Rose for Emily," critic Melinda Schwab writes:

> What would a woman like Emily Grierson, who seems to us fixed in the past and oblivious to any passing of time, need with a watch? An awareness of the significance of this watch, however, is crucial for a clear understanding of Miss Emily herself. The watch's placement in her pocket, its unusually loud ticking, and the chain to which it is attached illustrate both her attempts to control the passage of the years and the consequences of such an ultimately futile effort.

Imagine that a student wishes to include this information in his or her paper *exactly* as it appears in each box below. Read each example and consider what qualities make it legitimate or plagiarized.

Example 1

> A reader might wonder why a woman like Emily Grierson would need a watch. The watch's placement in her pocket, its unusually loud ticking, and the chain to which it is attached illustrate both her attempts to control the passage of the years and the consequences of such an ultimately futile effort.

This *is* plagiarism. There is no attempt to identify the source or to credit her words (using quotation marks). The student is copying the information and presenting it as his own.

Example 2

> Melinda Schwab first wonders why Emily needs a watch and then answers her own question: "The watch's placement in her pocket, its unusually loud ticking, and the chain to which it is attached illustrate both her attempts to control the passage of the years and the consequences of such an ultimately futile effort" (215).

This is *not* plagiarism. The source is identified and her words are credited in quotation marks. The page on which the quoted information appears is also provided. The student is citing responsibly.

Example 3

> Melinda Schwab first wonders why Emily Grierson needs a watch. She then argues that the watch's placement in her pocket, its strangely loud ticking, and the chain it is attached to illustrate her attempts to control the years' passing as well as the consequences of such an ultimately futile attempt (215).

Surprisingly, this *is* plagiarism. Although Schwab is properly credited for the *idea*, her *words* are copied nearly verbatim without proper credit. This is known as "tracing." If you're going to copy a source this closely—reproducing essentially the same sequence and flow of thoughts—then you must copy the original wording exactly as it appears and place it in quotation marks.

Example 4

> Melinda Schwab argues that examining the manner in which Emily closely holds her watch and even seems to keep it attached to her illuminates her doomed desires to control time (215).

This is *not* plagiarism. Unlike the previous example, this is a responsible and effective use of paraphrase. The source is credited for the idea, but the source's words have been converted to a significantly shorter and substantially different form. The quotation marks can be removed. The idea still belongs to Schwab, but it is now legitimately being expressed in the *student's* own words.

Example 5

> Examining the manner in which Emily closely holds her watch and even seems to keep it attached to her illuminates her doomed desire to control time.

This *is* plagiarism. Since the student has converted the source's words into a significantly shorter and substantially different form, he does not need to use quotation marks; however, he still needs to credit Schwab for the *idea*. If he added an introductory phrase—such as, "Melinda Schwab argues that…"—this would be a legitimate use of paraphrase. With no mention of Schwab, however, it is plagiarism.

MLA Citation

MLA citation may seem baffling, but there are good reasons for its rules. Knowing some of those *reasons* will make it easier to understand the many variations of citation.

There are four major reasons to cite sources: (1) To **justify** our own interpretations of literary texts by showing that they are supported by, or add productively to, an ongoing critical conversation about those texts; (2) to give **credit** to *words* and *ideas* which are not our own; (3) to establish our **credibility** by demonstrating our awareness of, and indebtedness to, other critics' views; and (4) to help readers **locate** those sources if they wish to consult them directly. To accomplish these ends, we need to identify *which text* we are citing and *where* the information can be found. MLA style provides this information via parenthetical citation and the Works Cited page.

Parenthetical Citation

Parenthetical citation lets the reader know, sentence-by-sentence, whenever *words* or *ideas* contained in your paper *did not originate with you*. If the words and ideas are yours, no parenthetical citation is needed. However, if you refer to words or ideas from a primary or secondary source, you must use parenthetical citation to show where this information came from.

In its simplest form, parenthetical citation provides two pieces of information:

1. the *last name of the author* from whom the information was borrowed
2. the *page(s)* on which the cited information appears (for poetry, use line numbers)

This information is called a "parenthetical citation" because it is cited in parentheses, immediately following the borrowed information. For example, if I quote from Nathaniel Hawthorne's short story "Young Goodman Brown," it might look like this:

> The story confronts readers with a difficult question: "Had Goodman Brown fallen asleep in the forest and only dreamed a wild dream of a witch-meeting?" (Hawthorne 89).

The quotation marks clarify which words are not mine. The parenthetical citation identifies the *author* of those words (Hawthorne) and the *page* of the story on which they appear (page 89).

Readers who wish to track down the original source will need additional information about the text I used. After all, Hawthorne's story has been published in many different places, and although every copy should contain the same quotation, it will not always be located on the same page. This is where the Works Cited page comes in.

Works Cited Page

The information on the Works Cited page helps your reader locate the same editions of the texts you cited in your paper by providing the full publication information. It should *begin on a new page* at the end of the paper, with the heading "Works Cited" centered at the top. The entire page is double-spaced, just like the rest of the essay, with no additional spaces inserted between each citation. Each citation begins at the left margin (not indented). If a citation runs longer than one full line, indent all subsequent lines 0.5 inches (one Tab).

There are too many possible variations to list, but here are a few of the most common types of sources formatted according to MLA style standards, seventh edition:

Text in an Anthology (Collection of Works)

Hawthorne, Nathaniel. "Young Goodman Brown." *Literature: The Human Experience*. Ed. Richard Abcarian and Marvin Klotz. Shorter 9th ed. Boston: Bedford/St. Martin's, 2007. 80-90. Print.

> Note: Short story and poem titles appear in quotation marks. Plays and book titles are italicized. The anthology title is italicized. The editors' names appear next, followed by the edition number (if present), the *first* listed city of publication, the publisher, the year of publication, the page range on which the text appears (here, pages 80 - 90), and the medium in which it was accessed (Print).

Single-Author Book (Literary or Scholarly)

Douglass, Frederick. *Narrative of the Life of Frederick Douglass*. Ed. John W. Blassingame, John R. McKivigan, and Peter P. Hinks. New Haven: Yale UP, 2001. Print.

> Note: Book titles are italicized. If there are three or fewer editors, list their names in full. If there are more than three, list only the first editor's name, followed by "et al."

Article in a Journal/Periodical (Accessed in Print)

Nebeker, Helen. E. "'The Lottery': Symbolic Tour de Force." *American Literature* 46.1 (1974): 100-08. Print.

> Note: The journal title is italicized. It is followed by the volume and issue number (here, volume 46, issue 1), the year of publication, the page range on which the article appears (here, pages 100 - 108), and the medium in which it was accessed (Print). If the volume is not divided into issues, the issue number is omitted.

Article in a Journal/Periodical (Accessed Electronically)

Nebeker, Helen E. "'The Lottery': Symbolic Tour de Force." *American Literature* 46.1 (1974): 100-08. *JSTOR*. Web. 10 Oct. 2008.

> Note: This article is available in print, but was accessed electronically through the JSTOR database. The Works Cited entry includes all of the print publication information *plus* the electronic access details: the database name (JSTOR), the medium in which it was accessed (Web), and the date it was accessed.

Revision: Refinement is a Process

Students tend to think "revision" is the same as "proofreading," but it involves a lot more than basic editing. Revision means "to see again" because the challenge of good writing is to envision other, better ways to express the same ideas—not just by "tweaking" words and sentences, but by restructuring whole paragraphs or series of paragraphs. The goals of revision are the same as the goals of effective writing in general: (1) clarity, (2) conciseness, and (3) style—in that order of importance.

Below is a sample paragraph analyzing Manley Pointer, the con-artist from Flannery O'Connor's story "Good Country People." The student is trying to describe some of the story's earliest clues that Manley is not the naïve, Bible-selling country boy he pretends to be. Most readers overlook these clues, which are subtle and scattered several paragraphs apart. The challenge is to gather these clues together and present them in a clear manner so the reader will recognize them as clear warning signs about Manley's character. Moreover, the reader needs to be convinced that these clues are concretely observable, not based on a fuzzy gut-feeling or sheer speculation without evidence.

Watch how the paragraph evolves through five drafts in order to become truly "polished":

Draft 1 (282 words / quality: D)

One of the warning signs that Manley is not an honest Bible salesman is seen when he says his first word in the story. "Good morning, Mrs. Cedars!" he says to Mrs. Hopewell (104). She corrects him and tells him her real name. By this it would seem that he knew nothing about Mrs. Hopewell or her daughter. However, soon after Manley says, "I know ... you're a good woman. Friends have told me" (105). From this it can be assumed that he knows more than he first let on about Mrs. Hopewell. If he knew that she was a good woman, he would at the very least know her name, but he is trying to seem innocently simple. If this is the case, then he may be trying to play to her presumption that "good country people" are simple but trustworthy, and make her believe that he is indeed simple by assuming her name was the name on the mailbox (101). "'Oh!' He said, pretending to look puzzled but with eyes sparkling, 'I saw it said "The Cedars," on the mailbox so I thought you was Mrs. Cedars!'" (104). He continues this "good country person" facade when he says, "I know I'm real simple. I don't know how to say a thing but to say it. I'm just a country boy.... People like you don't like to fool with country people like me!" (105). To which Mrs. Hopewell replies, "Why ... good country people are the salt of the earth! Besides, we all have different ways of doing, it takes all kinds to make the world go 'round. That's life!" (105). At this point Manley has her in his deceitful grasp.

This draft contains the right kind of textual evidence, but far too much of it. Much of this is unnecessary, even if it is mildly relevant. It feels cluttered and verbose, and the central point is not explained clearly.

Draft 2 (190 words / quality: low C)

When Manley is introduced halfway into the story, he leads Mrs. Hopewell to believe he is just a country boy just trying to sell bibles to people. When Manley first speaks he says to Mrs. Hopewell "Good Morning, Mrs. Cedars!" (104). Mrs. Hopewell then informs him of her real name and he says that he saw the name Cedars on the mailbox so that is why he was mistaken (104). As the story goes on, Manley starts trying to convince Mrs. Hopewell to buy a bible. He says to her: "I know you believe in Chrustian service ... I know ... you're a good woman. Friends have told me" (105). I think that this is odd because when he first came to the door, Manley did not even know Mrs. Hopewell's name. But then he sits down to talk to Mrs. Hopewell about buying bibles and suddenly he reveals that he knows she is a Christian because friends have informed him of that fact. I believe this is not just a coincidence that Manley happens to know what her interests are but has no idea what Mrs. Hopewell's name is.

This draft wisely condenses the evidence by eliminating or paraphrasing non-essential information; however, it describes the evidence in extremely vague language ("not just a coincidence"). Readers are left to form their own conclusions, so the writer is not really in control of the analysis and its conclusions.

Draft 3 (132 words / quality: C)

Manley's initial sign of deception is revealed when he first encounters Mrs. Hopewell at the front door. He pretends to act surprised and puzzled when he calls her by the wrong name from the mailbox. "'Oh!' he said, pretending to look puzzled" (104). Not only does he show that he is fake by pretending to be puzzled, but he also lies in the very same instance. He pretends not to know Mrs. Hopewell, yet later he claims to know she is a good woman and that she believes in "Chrustian" service because "Friends have told me" (105). This shows that he must have had prior knowledge of Mrs. Hopewell and maybe even Joy, otherwise how could he mistake her for Mrs. Cedars if he has already asked around about Mrs. Hopewell's character?

This evidence is better focused, but still presented awkwardly. The quote is dropped in without context. Thanks to greater emphasis on the word "pretending," the central point is becoming clearer, but it is presented in the very weak form of a question. Analysis should provide answers, not ask questions.

Draft 4 (157 words / quality: B)

> Manley's deceit is evident when he first meets Mrs. Hopewell and feigns surprise that her name does not match the name on her mailbox: "'Oh!' he said, pretending to look puzzled ... 'I saw it said "The Cedars" on the mailbox so I thought you was Mrs. Cedars!'" (104). The word "pretending" suggests Manley is being deliberately dishonest, and this is confirmed when he later tells Mrs. Hopewell: "I know ... you're a good woman. Friends have told me" (105). It is impossible that Manley has asked friends about Mrs. Hopewell's character ahead of time if, as he claimed earlier, he mistakenly believed her name was Mrs. Cedars. One of these sentiments must be a lie. Since he also makes an extremely unlikely claim to have a "heart condition" like Joy-Hulga, the only possible conclusion is that he has been stalking the Hopewells to find a way to ingratiate himself so he can steal Joy-Hulga's peg leg.

This draft lengthens the quote to clarify context, and states its claim directly: "One of these sentiments is a lie." Now the tone is confident and the reader cannot fail to understand what the evidence is showing.

Draft 5 (131 words / quality: A)

> Manley's deceit is evident when he first greets Mrs. Hopewell with surprise that her name does not match the name on her mailbox: "'Oh!' he said, *pretending* to look puzzled ... 'I saw ... the mailbox so I thought you was Mrs. Cedars!'" (104, emphasis added). This depiction of Manley as a pretender is confirmed when he later tells Mrs. Hopewell: "I know ... you're a good woman. Friends have told me" (105). If Manley truly mistook her for Mrs. Cedars, he could not have asked friends about her character. One of these sentiments is a lie. Since, in an almost impossible coincidence, he also claims to share Joy-Hulga's "heart condition," the probable truth is that he has been studying the Hopewells for a way to ingratiate himself to steal Joy-Hulga's prosthetic leg.

This draft intelligently shortens the quotation (yet retains enough for context), and adds italic emphasis to "pretending" to highlight O'Connor's significant word choice. (Notice that the parenthetical citation must show that the italic emphasis was added by the student, not O'Connor.) Also, minor errors are corrected ("peg leg" is corrected to "prosthetic leg") and falsely overstated claims ("only possible conclusion") are prudently softened ("probable truth") to maintain credibility.

The Drafting Process

Think carefully about the gradual process of refinement that occurs from draft to draft. From Draft 1 to 4, there is a remarkable improvement. The first three drafts seem verbose because they lack clear focus and handle evidence (quotations) awkwardly. The central idea is present and partly coherent, but it doesn't sound clear and persuasive because the logic and flow of the paragraph are still rough. This is especially apparent at the end of drafts 2 and 3. Draft 2 merely observes that the discrepancies in Manley's claims are "just not a coincidence" and Draft 3 expresses this sentiment more fully, but in the weak form of a question, rather than as a confident claim. In both of these cases, readers are never actually told how to interpret Manley; instead, they are left to draw their conclusions.

In Drafts 4 and 5, the tone is much more confident because the writer's thought process is stated directly and explicitly: "One of these sentiments must be a lie." Now the writer is asserting real *control* over the reader's mind, pushing readers to reach precisely the conclusions that the writer wants them to reach. As long as sufficient evidence accompanies these claims, readers will appreciate—rather than resist—this kind of directness. Obviously, readers want to know precisely what the writer thinks and why; otherwise, they would read something else!

Now think about how much more credibility and persuasive power *your words* will have if you are willing to invest the effort and patience required for your ideas to evolve to this sophisticated degree. It is a slow and tedious process initially, but if you stick with serious draft-to-draft revision, you will eventually learn to articulate yourself in a truly powerful way. Then you will begin to command far greater respect among your peers, professors, and employers.

Conclusion

Many students fill out the conclusion with generic, sentimental, and idealistic statements or clichés that have little or nothing to do with the preceding discussion in the body of the paper. This is unfortunate because a poor conclusion can sabotage what otherwise might have been an outstanding paper.

Structurally, you can think of the conclusion as a reverse-introduction, with slightly higher stakes. Whereas the introduction flows from *general* premises and observations toward a *specific* claim (thesis), the conclusion flows the opposite direction: from a *specific* claim (usually, a restatement of the thesis) toward more *general* observations about the value and applicability of that claim to the work as a whole.

A strong conclusion should:

- **remind the reader of your central argument**
  The conclusion should restate the thesis—not in exactly the same language, but in a form that closely echoes the original thesis. This reminds the reader of the paper's major claims. This should be easier than writing the introduction because the reader now has the benefit of having read your argument in full. Try to sum up your views clearly and concisely.

- **bring a sense of closure to your essay**
  The conclusion should *not* introduce new evidence or advance new claims beyond the scope of the thesis; otherwise, the paper will feel "unfinished" and leave the reader dissatisfied. The conclusion should reassure the reader that the paper has "made good" on whatever the thesis promised. Usually, this is best accomplished by reminding the reader of your central argument (see above) and clarifying the importance of that argument (see below).

- **clarify the importance of your argument**
  The conclusion should explain why your argument is productive and insightful. One way to do this is to crisply and efficiently summarize the flow of the arguments presented in the body of the paper, followed by concise explanations of how these arguments enrich our appreciation of the meaning of the text(s) as a whole. The conclusion may also briefly allude to new issues that deserve further consideration, but only if those issues *arise directly and logically from the claims you have just presented, are not phrased as claims*, and *do not require explanation to establish their relevance or importance.*

Never use clichés or vague generalizations in your conclusion, no matter how "witty" or "profound" they seem to you. Your paper has already laid out the argument and evidence you wish to pursue, so your conclusion should articulate those ideas clearly and concisely, not in generic terms. Explain, in specific language, the value of the argument that you have offered and how it matters to our understanding of the text as a whole.

Never begin your conclusion with awkwardly formal phrases, such as, "in conclusion" or "to sum up." Instead, ease into your concluding paragraph with a more elegant transition sentence that neatly summarizes the gist of what the preceding body paragraphs have shown. Your reader already knows that the last paragraph is the conclusion, so there is no need to state it so conspicuously.

Formatting

College essays follow simple, practical formatting guidelines. Disregarding these guidelines may make you appear lazy, apathetic, or discourteous to your professors and will almost certainly result in a lower grade. If you want your work to be taken seriously, you cannot afford to neglect these basic elements of professionalism.

Here are the formatting guidelines that academic papers are normally expected to follow:

- **Staple the pages together**
  Staple your essay with a single staple in the upper-left corner. Do not "dog-ear" or paper-clip the pages. Not stapling your paper is one of the surest ways to annoy your professor.

- **Do not use protective or decorative covers**
  Do not use a protective or decorative cover for your essay. The extra weight and bulk are inconvenient when professors have to carry a stack of student essays.

- **Set all margins to one inch**
  Padded margins look lazy and suggest that you think the professor is too stupid to notice.

- **Use Times New Roman font, size 12**
  This is the standard academic font. Do not use a different font without permission.

- **Include a proper heading**
  Identify *your name*, your *professor's name*, the *course title/section*, and the *date submitted*, each on a separate line at the top of your essay (left-aligned, double-spaced).

- **Include a short, descriptive title**
  Give your essay a brief title that concisely describes the topic or main idea of your essay. The title is centered, in the same font as the rest of the essay, not bolded or underlined.

- **Do not insert extra space (line breaks) above or below the title**
  The title should be one double-spaced line below the heading and one double-spaced line above the introduction. Do not insert extra space.

- **Do not add extra space between paragraphs**
  Paragraphs are distinguished by normal indentation. Do not insert additional line breaks above or below them.

- **Include page numbers**
  The header of every page contains your last name and the page number (right-aligned).

- **Do not shortchange or exceed the page limit**
  Professors set page limits for good reasons. Do not turn in less or more than requested. *Revise* to make your ideas developed and concise enough to fit within the limits.

- **Begin the list of Works Cited on a new page**
  Even if there is leftover space on the last page of your essay, insert a page-break to start the list of Works Cited on a new page. Center the words "Works Cited" at the top of the page and cite your primary and secondary sources in correct MLA style.

Writing Tips

These valuable tips will help you to improve your writing and to avoid common errors:

- **Write in present tense**
  Past tense sounds stale. Present tense sounds fresher and more engaging, as if the author and the reader are examining the evidence together, in the here and now.

  > Past: In *Paradise Lost*, Milton showed how man was first tempted to sin. This sin was a voluntary choice on man's part. Milton's point was that man chose his own fate and had to live with the consequences.

  > Present: In *Paradise Lost*, Milton shows how man is first tempted to sin. This sin is voluntary on man's part. Milton's point is that man chooses his own fate and must live with the consequences.

- **Avoid the familiar "you"**
  Use formal/general references to "the reader" or "the audience" instead of directly addressing the reader with the familiar "you," which feels coercive and may alienate the reader.

  > Direct/Familiar: You cannot read the title of the story "Good Country People" without instantly thinking of the uneducated 'country bumpkin' stereotype. O'Connor deliberately sets you up to realize that you share some of Joy-Hulga's arrogance. (The reader may respond: *That's not true! Stop telling me how my mind works!*)

  > Formal/General: Most readers cannot read the title of the story "Good Country People" without instantly thinking of the uneducated 'country bumpkin' stereotype. O'Connor deliberately sets up readers to realize that they share some of Joy-Hulga's arrogance. (The reader may respond: *Okay, I'll accept that—although I don't personally react that way.*)

- **Remove personal qualifiers** ("I believe," "I think," "in my opinion," etc.)
  Anything *you* argue is obviously *your* belief, *your* thought, *your* opinion. There's no need to keep reminding us. Your writing will sound more confident without such qualifiers.

  > With qualifiers: I think Huck realizes that Jim deserves to be free. In my opinion, Huck understands that slavery is unfair.

  > Without qualifiers: Huck realizes that Jim should be free. Huck understands that slavery is unfair.

- **Be concise**
  Don't use ten words if five will suffice.

  > Verbose: When Joy's leg is taken from her at the end of the story, she doesn't know what to do with herself because she is so reliant on her leg which makes the audience see a very different side of Joy.

  > Concise: When Joy's leg is stolen at the end of the story, we see a very different side of her.

- **Avoid clichés**
  Clichés undermine the precision and force of your writing. Avoid trite phrases like these:

  > little does he know, icing on the cake, sneaking suspicion, blind leading the blind, playing with fire, bright and shining, loud and clear, but I digress, calm before the storm, blessing in disguise, gets the last laugh, more than meets the eye, what goes around comes around, etc.

- **Minimize summary**
  Summary should only be used if it is absolutely necessary to clarify your argument. Even then, it should be *brief* (a sentence or two) and should *work in service to a strong claim*. Never summarize the main plot. Assume your professor has read the text.

- **Eliminate contractions**
  Contractions are too informal for academic writing. Instead of *isn't, aren't, haven't,* or other common contractions, use their proper forms: *is not, are not, have not,* etc.

- **Eliminate "wimpy verbs"** (is, am, are, was, were, be, being, been)
  "Wimpy verbs" typically surface in the passive voice. If you eliminate them, your writing will favor the active voice, which is clearer, more concise, and more confident.

  > Passive voice (wimpy): The lamp was broke by Tom while he was swinging the cat by the tail. Now he is afraid of being grounded by dad.

  > Active voice (strong): Tom swung the cat by the tail and broke the lamp. Now he fears that dad will ground him.

- **Eliminate rhetorical questions**
  Rhetorical questions do not belong in an academic essay. They waste space, irritate your reader, and obscure your meaning. Rather than ask questions, your paper should provide *answers* by stating your views directly, which is always clearer and more concise.

  > Rhetorical: I feel as though this critic could have done a better job presenting the fact that why would a man pursue a woman if he is not romantically interested?

  > Direct: This critic should have clarified why a man would pursue a woman if he lacks romantic interest.

  > Rhetorical: Is Shakespeare suggesting that Kate has been utterly transformed in response to Petruccio's harsh treatment? It seems unlikely.

  > Direct: It seems unlikely that Kate has been utterly transformed in response to Petruccio's harsh treatment

- **Avoid references to movies, songs, or other forms of "pop culture"**
  Unless your professor explicitly gives you permission to do so, never compare a literary text to a movie, song, or other form of pop culture. This is a sure way to wander off-topic, undermine your credibility, and shortchange legitimate analysis.

- **Eliminate vague sentiments — especially words like "interesting" or "meaningful"**
  Vague statements seriously undermine your credibility and persuasive power.

  > Vague: I found Smith's viewpoint very interesting and it helped me to look at this story in a more meaningful way. This sentence says nothing. It should explain *why* the viewpoint is interesting and *how* it makes the story more meaningful.

  > Meaningful: Smith's view calls vital attention to the fact that Arnold Friend may be a mere figment of Connie's imagination, in which case Oates's story has more to say about teen angst, than about the dangers of serial rape and murder.

- **Eliminate ideas that exceed the scope of your essay**
  Your essay should never include cursory observations such as: Another reason for this view is the complex chronology of the story, which is a whole other essay topic. This remark is pointless. It mentions a vague idea which, by the writer's own admission, lies beyond the scope of the essay. Ideas must be discussed and developed; otherwise, they have no place in your essay.

- **Read your paper aloud**
  Your ear will detect mechanical and grammatical errors that your eyes miss. Read your paper aloud from beginning to end, and you will hear or stumble over many of these rough spots. Keep revising until you can read smoothly through the entire paper.

12843373R00032

Made in the USA
San Bernardino, CA
28 June 2014